THE TRIUMPHANT EXISTENCE

THE TRIUMPHANT EXISTENCE

Biblical Advice for Revitalizing Your Life

Lee Franklin

Triple Up Publications

Printed in the United States of America

First Printing, 2016

ISBN 0-9896279-0-X

Triple Up Publications
P.O. Box 7952
Columbia, MO 65205

DEDICATION

For Jayden and Jeremiah

CONTENTS

INTRODUCTION

The Bible has always been an important part of my life. I grew up going to church every Sunday and was taught that if you need something, you should ask God. I always believed that when all else failed, prayer would work; but the older I grew, the more I questioned things. If something did not make sense, I was the first to point it out and I looked for inconsistencies in everything.

When I took a look at religions, most of the focus seemed to revolve around the afterlife. It seemed the ultimate question was, How can we and others make it to heaven and have eternal life? There is nothing wrong with that, but I also wanted to know how I could make this life better.

This took me on a mini journey, during which I studied various religions and philosophies that have arisen throughout human history. I studied with Buddhists, Muslims, Christians, Jews, Hebrew-Israelites, agnostics, Afrocentrists and atheists. I scoured the Bible, the Koran, the Book of Mormon, the Pseudepigrapha, the Apocrypha, the I Ching, and the Talmud. I also studied the various religions of antiquity as I looked for similarities, inaccuracies, and helpful advice.

All of this searching took me 360 degrees—right back to the Bible. Some people might chalk this up to me being biased toward the Bible due to my upbringing. However, I truly found the Bible to be the best source for practical advice on making this life better. I believe God had me take this long, circuitous route in order to bring me back to this book. It is this journey that gave me an even more strengthened view of the Bible and allowed me to write this book.

I believe that God cares very much about our lives here on Earth. The Bible gives both spiritual and practical advice for our physical lives; in fact, some things that are taught in the Bible can be applicable to both. This makes sense, as our spiritual and natural lives are connected. One thing you can ask yourself is, What kind of life do you think God truly wants for you? Does he want you to have a life filled with misery or one that is happy? Would he prefer you to have a pessimistic outlook or one that is optimistic? Jesus had an optimistic outlook. His message and works were encouraging and he forgave and saw the best in people. This is the type of life we should want to lead.

Far too many people have expectations of hard times; this causes us to live restricted lives. We justify our hard times as God testing us. While it may be true that God is testing us, we often bring these hardships upon ourselves. Many of these self-created hardships can be overcome by heeding the advice that the Bible gives us.

That is what this book is about—practical biblical advice on how to get the most out of our lives and make it better. Bible verses are quoted and then I explain how they can be applied to our lives. In order to fully explain them, I use examples of successful people with whom you may be familiar. I also draw on a few examples from my life. The personal examples mainly revolve around my experience of teaching in China and my participation in sports; I have both played and coached football. These references and examples help to fully paint the picture.

One thing to note—this book is not about a certain dogma. I am a teacher by profession. I believe I am meant to teach, not pastor or preach. Pastoring should be left to your pastor. This book is written to teach you ways to improve this gift of physical life that God has given you.

This book can benefit anyone who is looking to improve his or her life. I must be clear though: Simply reading this book will not change your life. Learning and APPLYING these basic principles will. This book is intended to be easy to grasp. Everyone can understand its principles; it is up to you to apply them. Nothing in your life will change until you change. Insanity is repeating the same action again and again and expecting different results. You can continue living the same life, or you can choose to take action to revitalize your life. Reading this book is the first step.

Hopefully, everyone reading this book can get something of value out of it. Everyone has the God-given potential to be great. It is the mastering of the basics that makes one great. This book strives to get us back to the basics in the Bible and the basics of life. There is nothing more basic than love. This book was written with love. God is love. You, too, should operate out of love.

Read this book. Study this book. Learn the principles and apply them to your life. If you do that, God will improve your life. You deserve to live a long, exciting and triumphant life filled with joy.

-Lee Franklin

1 GO TO THE ANT

Proverbs 6:6 – *Go to the ant, O sluggard; consider her ways, and be wise.*

We all took notice of ants when we were kids. We noticed how they seemed to be on the same page as each other, and how they carried food to the dirt nests that they built. Ants are known as diligent, hard workers. They represent the opposite of laziness. When the Bible tells us to consider the ant and be wise, it is telling us not to be lazy.

As young students in school, we heard the famous Aesop's fable of the grasshopper and the ant. The grasshopper was relaxing during the summer while the ants were preparing food for the winter. The grasshopper thought he could sleep a little bit, do the work near the summer's end, and still be okay. Suffice it to say, he was ill-prepared when winter came. The ants, on the other hand, had enough food stored for the winter due to their hard work.

Aesop was a wise man. King Solomon, too, was known as a wise man—the wisest in the world. He is generally recognized as being an author of the book of Proverbs, in which he gives advice that is identical to Aesop's.

Proverbs 20:4 – The sluggard does not plow in the autumn; he will seek at harvest and have nothing.

Both of these wise men warned of doing work now so that we can be secure when it is time to harvest and reap. They say great minds think alike, and two of the most recognizable wise men in history give the same advice— don't be lazy!

The Bible speaks very negatively of laziness. It says that the lazy man gets nothing. It links laziness with poverty and likens it to wasting time. It even goes as far as suggesting that slothfulness kills.

Proverbs 21:25 – The desire of the sluggard kills him, for his hands refuse to labor.

Proverbs 10:5 – *He who gathers in summer is a prudent son, but he who sleeps in harvest is a son who brings shame.*

Proverbs 18:9 – *Whoever is slack in his work is a brother to him who destroys.*

Laziness truly does get you nothing. If you look at successful people, no matter what their field or profession, one thing you will notice is that they are not lazy. They often put in more work than the average person. They have failed many times like all of us, but the thing that separates them from everyone else is that they keep working. No matter how many times they have failed before, they keep going.

We have heard the various stories of our heroes. Michael Jordan was cut from his high school basketball team before becoming arguably the greatest basketball player of all time. Reggie Miller had leg braces when he was a kid. He overcame that obstacle to become a Hall of Fame basketball player known for his sharpshooting. Henry Ford was told by his engineers that the Model T was not plausible. Julius Caesar cried in front of the statue of Alexander the Great due to his lack of success; he then went on to conquer the known world. Thomas Edison failed over 1,000 times before successfully inventing the lightbulb. Edison said he never failed; rather, he found a thousand ways not to do it. These are just a few examples of people overcoming the odds and becoming successful. Like the ant, the key to their success was diligence and hard work.

Proverbs 12:24 – The hand of the diligent will rule, while the slothful will be put to forced labor.

We all want to make money, have good health, be successful in our careers, and accomplish our goals. More often than not, we become lazy and lax with regard to these aspects of our lives. Why is one person successful and another not? Many factors can play into this; however, one factor—perhaps the strongest factor—is the level of diligence and perseverance we put into our task. When we were younger, it seemed like everyone wanted to be a professional athlete, a famous singer or actor, a doctor, or a lawyer. For most people, those dreams never materialized beyond talk. When we grow up, our goals also become all talk—but talk alone gets us nowhere.

Proverbs 14:23 - In all toil there is profit, but mere talk tends only to poverty.

Eventually, we are going to have to put our money where our mouth is. That means taking consistent action.

Laziness is the biggest hindrance to achieving our goals. Other people, obstacles, and situations can hold us back only to the extent that we let them. Usually, we are really the ones to blame. If we break situations down, we will notice that many times we hurt our chances through laziness, lack of motivation, and the desire to be constantly entertained.

Success requires great discipline. Tasks need to be carried out expediently and efficiently and sometimes sacrifices have to be made. Those who are great at what they do often sacrifice their time. In the off-season, it has been said that Kobe Bryant would take 700– 1,000 shots a day in order to perfect his rhythm. He and other successful people have learned to discipline themselves. Disciplining yourself is not easy, but it is rewarding.

Hebrews 12:11 – *For the moment all discipline seems painful rather than pleasant, but later it yields the peaceful fruit of righteousness to those who have been trained by it.*

Why is disciplining ourselves not easy? It is because a little leaven leavens the whole lump.

I Corinthians 5:6 – *Your boasting is not good. Do you not know that a little leaven leavens the whole lump?*

What does that mean? To explain, think about this: we have all started a diet or exercise regimen on fire, only to lose the initial excitement after a little while. When we are consistently on task, we feel good. However, it is missing that one day that sets us back. After that day, it gets easier to take another day off. Eventually, our whole regimen ends up collapsing and we fail to achieve our goal. That little leaven—that little rest—hurt our whole lump/progress.

Proverbs 24:33–34 – *A little sleep, a little slumber, a little folding of the hands to rest, and poverty will come upon you like a robber, and want like an armed man.*

Instant gratification is a killer. We want pleasure now. We want to relax this day, watch this show, and go to this party instead of working on the task at hand. This is not to say we should never relax or have fun. Quite the contrary, we should enjoy life. However, if we have a goal and a task that needs to be done, we should prioritize. Esau is an example of someone in the Bible who did not prioritize. One day, after returning from hunting, he was hungry. Not thinking about the long term, he traded his birthright to his brother for some food.

Hebrews 12:16-17 – *that no one is sexually immoral or unholy like Esau, who sold his birthright for a single meal. For you know that afterward, when he desired to inherit the blessing, he was rejected, for he found no chance to repent, though he sought it with tears.*

Esau wanted instant gratification. It is easy to talk about how silly of a decision Esau made and to believe that we would never make such a ridiculous choice. The thing is, though, that we trade future success for instant gratification all the time. Stay disciplined! The Bible tells us that we should go about our endeavors diligently and with might.

Ecclesiastes 9:10-11 – *Whatever your hand finds to do, do it with your might, for there is no work or thought or knowledge or wisdom in Sheol, to which you are going. Again I saw that under the sun the race is not to the swift, nor the battle to the strong, nor bread to the wise, nor riches to the intelligent, nor favor to those with knowledge, but time and chance happen to them all.*

This verse above is very important and telling. Whatever you do, make sure you do it right and with might. Do it diligently. The battle is not given to the rich or the strong; rather, success is given to those who notice their opportunity and work at it. When opportunity knocks, recognize it and be willing to break the door down to let it in. It *will* knock. Time and chance happen to us all. We need to make sure we hear it and do our tasks as if we are doing them for God.

Colossians 3:17 – *And whatever you do, in word or deed, do everything in the name of the Lord Jesus, giving thanks to God the Father through him.*

I love to watch track and field during the Olympics. When they are having a race, all of the runners in the race run, but only one gets the gold medal. Run the race in life in order to get the gold medal. Remember, in all things, it is those that endure until the end; those that see their tasks through to completion and fruition that triumph. Do not be a lazy sluggard. Be a hardworking, goal-oriented, on-task ant!

I Corinthians 9:24 – *Do you not know that in a race all the runners run, but only one receives the prize? So run that you may obtain it.*

Matthew 24:13 – *But the one who endures to the end will be saved.*

2 AS A MAN THINKS

Proverbs 23:7 – *For as he thinks in his heart, so is he*

The way we think is very important. Our thinking is an intricate part of our lives. Our thoughts make us who we are and our minds are very revealing. However, our actions can be faked. Someone can pretend to be tough on the outside, while really being scared on the inside. Our thoughts are the controlling factor. Most of the time, we do not control our thoughts. Sometimes, our thoughts control us without us being consciously aware of it. This is called an involuntary response. Breathing is a basic example of this. We need to learn how to control, correct, and direct our minds. Mastering this can be one of our biggest assets.

Proverbs 4:23 – *Keep your heart with all vigilance, for from it flow the springs of life.*

Think about this: If most people were to wake up to $100,000 in their bank account, they would be ecstatic! However, if a billionaire were to wake up to $1,000,000 in his account, he would probably become depressed and despondent. Why the drastic difference? The depressed ex-billionaire still has ten times more money than the ecstatic person.

The difference is in their thinking. Everything is relative, including our thinking. One sees an opportunity, while the other sees losses. For both of these people, this would be a natural thought process. These two people are in different situations: the ex-billionaire is despondent because he has been used to having much more money, while the other person is excited because he has not had that type of money before.

Both people should alter their thinking. The billionaire should lose the sadness and work on how he can build his funds back up. The one with $100,000 can be excited, but then he needs to think of ways to put his money to good use. In every situation, we should try to see the positive—the light at the end of the tunnel. This takes effort but can be done if we believe that everything happens for a reason and that all things work together for good. Be an optimist and see the glass half full.

Romans 8:28 – And we know that for those who love God all things work together for good, for those who are called according to his purpose.

Our thoughts are our true prayers. We will pray for something but take no action to get it because we do not truly believe that our prayers will be answered. Our actions reveal our thoughts. Every action starts as a thought, whether it is voluntary or involuntary. Our thoughts and actions go hand in hand.

Our thoughts do not just control our actions; our actions manipulate our thoughts as well. If we can get a sad person to smile for us, even if the person has to force it out, he/she will feel a little bit better. The person will not feel completely better, but smiling will make him/her feel better to a degree. This is an example of our action manipulating our thinking. In sports, we would repeat an action until it became second nature for us. We could perform the action in the game without consciously thinking about it.

If we are feeling down, we can change that thinking. If we feel poor, we can change that thinking too.

We can change the outlook of our situation and eventually change the actual situation. This is not easy and it takes practice. If we cannot pay for food, it is hard to think positive. Know, however, that if we want to change our situation, we must take the responsibility upon ourselves to change it. No one is going to do it for us; we have to bear our own load. If after we do all we can, we still cannot change the situation, maybe we need to change ourselves. In this way, we are often our own greatest enemy. We keep thinking nothing is going to change, so we do not take action. Things will never get better with that mentality. We must take responsibility and have the mentality that we will change our situation.

Galatians 6:5 – *For each will have to bear his own load.*

Train your mind to believe you can succeed at your endeavor despite the many stumbling blocks that will arise. Keep your mind on positive things. Our minds attract things to our lives. If you continue to focus on negative things, they will not go away. If you think, pray, believe, and act on succeeding, eventually you will be successful. Be steadfast and mentally tough. Think that you will accomplish your goal or die in the process.

Matthew 24:13 – *But the one who endures to the end will be saved.*

Negative thinking cannot produce positive results. I used to think about how much I hated my job. This would cause me to put in less than my full effort. How could I hope to be successful in that situation? I had to change my thinking. Only good thoughts bear good fruit. You sow what you reap. Sow good seeds.

Galatians 6:7 – *Do not be deceived: God is not mocked, for whatever one sows, that will he also reap.*

Matthew 7:17-18 – *So, every healthy tree bears good fruit, but the diseased tree bears bad fruit. A healthy tree cannot bear bad fruit, nor can a diseased tree bear good fruit.*

Some of us have had the same mentality for years. As I said in the Introduction, insanity is trying the same thing again and again and expecting different results. To get different results, we should change our thinking and actions. It is easy to get trapped in a mindset, and difficult to get out of one. We can become imprisoned in a mindset. This is why people sell drugs. It is not because they want to break the law. It is because that is the only way they can think to improve their situation. We do not change until our thinking changes.

Some people are taught to have a positive outlook. One person can blow a million dollars and become broke in a summer. Meanwhile, someone else can inherit a million dollars and triple that money. That is because the inheritor may have been taught the right mentality when it comes to money and him/herself. This is why there are families that have generational wealth. These people have a positive outlook and believe they will be successful. They then take measures to be successful. While this mentality may be easy for them to adopt due to their situation, it is a mentality that we can all possess.

Take, for instance, the countless number of rags-to-riches stories—John D. Rockefeller, Andrew Carnegie, Oprah Winfrey, Jim Carrey, Jay-Z, Ralph Lauren, and Sheldon Adelson, to name a few. Even though they were not raised around money, they were still able to possess the skills, gain the knowledge, and learn the rules of money in order to become—and stay—successful. They all had to learn to think and believe that they would be successful. In fact, Andrew Carnegie was the inspiration behind Napoleon Hill's famous book, *Think and Grow Rich*. All of them are proof that we can possess the right mentality despite being poor.

The "beauty and the beast" example is further proof that the right mindset will help us to be successful. Have you ever seen an average or below-average-looking guy with a gorgeous girlfriend or wife? We would ask ourselves or our friends how he ended up with her. This guy is able to win her heart because he has the correct thought process. He truly believes he can win her heart. That mentality causes him to exude confidence. Even though this man is below-average looking, he is able to be successful with a woman who is perceived to be "out of his league" because he possesses the right mindset. That mindset allows him to carry himself in a way that makes him desirable to the woman.

If all of these people—rich, poor, unattractive, beautiful, etc.—can possess the correct mindset, then you can too. Our minds are a powerful, God-given tool. There are people who have tried for years to lose weight or quit smoking. They tried all the current diets, exercises, gums, patches, etc. to no avail. However, for one reason or another, they wake up one day determined, no matter what, to accomplish their goal. From that day on, the person trying to lose weight begins to actually do so and keep it off. From that day on, the smoker quits cold turkey. These people wanted and tried for some time to live that healthier life, but they were not successful until they had the mental resolve to transform their situation.

Romans 12:2 – *Do not be conformed to this world, but be transformed by the renewal of your mind, that by testing you may discern what is the will of God, what is good and acceptable and perfect.*

In order to change our situation, we must eliminate fear from our thinking. Have you ever wanted to talk to someone you were attracted to, only to let fear stop you? Yes, me too. Fear can prevent us from accomplishing our goals. A little fear can be healthy as long as we do not let it hold us back from positive ventures.

Hebrews13:6 – *So we can confidently say, "The Lord is my helper; I will not fear; what can man do to me?"*

Fear occurs naturally in us all and it can cause us to make the wrong decision. Until we learn to control our thoughts, we should keep in mind that our hearts—how we feel—can deceive us. Use your knowledge, wisdom, reasoning, and logic. Thinking things through will help you make the correct decision.

Proverbs 28:26 – *Whoever trusts in his own mind is a fool, but he who walks in wisdom will be delivered.*

Jeremiah 17:9 – The heart is deceitful above all things, and desperately sick; who can understand it?

Whatever endeavor you undertake, you must think positive. Educate yourself, work hard, believe in the skills God gave you, and, no matter how many times you fail, never give up. The more you fail, the closer you are to success. God made you great. Believe that! Even Jesus said you can do greater things than he did. You have to be great for that!

John 14:12 – Truly, truly, I say to you, whoever believes in me will also do the works that I do; and greater works than these will he do, because I am going to the Father.

Proverbs 24:16 – for the righteous falls seven times and rises again, but the wicked stumble in times of calamity.

Philippians 4:8 – Finally, brothers, whatever is true, whatever is honorable, whatever is just, whatever is pure, whatever is lovely, whatever is commendable, if there is any excellence, if there is anything worthy of praise, think about these things.

3 YOUR BODY IS A TEMPLE

I Corinthians 6:19-20 – *Or do you not know that your body is a temple of the Holy Spirit within you, whom you have from God? You are not your own, for you were bought with a price. So glorify God in your body.*

In this chapter, Paul is discussing various sins and how to keep away from them. During the writing of this letter, he drops an idea with which some people may not be familiar—our bodies are a temple. Paul is not the only person in the Bible to describe our bodies as a temple. Jesus talked to his disciples and other people about how he was going to rebuild the temple in three days. The people were confused. They talked about the fact that it took forty-six long years to build this grand structure. Now this guy was supposed to rebuild it in three days? However, Jesus was talking about something different; he was talking about the temple of his physical body.

John 2:21 – But he was speaking about the temple of his body.

The two most influential people in the New Testament described the physical body as a temple. But what exactly is a temple? A temple is regarded as a place that has within it a divine presence and is reserved for a highly valued function. It is a place to be revered and respected—a place in which God dwells. Our bodies—our temples—are a place that should be taken care of and treated with high regard.

Besides a few verses describing our bodies as a temple, does the Bible tell us we should take care of our bodies? Yes! Even in the Old Testament, many of the laws were in place to keep the body healthy. Eating and drinking is a part of our daily lives, but the Bible tells us to eat and drink in a way that glorifies God.

I Corinthians 10:31 – So, whether you eat or drink, or whatever you do, do all to the glory of God.

I do believe in enjoying this God-given gift of life to the fullest. This means taking care of ourselves. We may not know what God has in store for us in the future. For example, we may want to be around for our grandchildren. It would be much better if we started taking care of ourselves now rather than later. We take years off our lives by not taking care of our bodies. Some people believe that, regardless of their efforts, they will die when it is their time. While it is true that we will all die at some point, that does not mean we should speed it along. We are supposed to reach old age. The Bible calls that a blessing.

Proverbs 16:31 – Gray hair is a crown of glory; it is gained in a righteous life.

Physical health also positively affects our mental well-being. Studies show that physical activity can be a great stress reliever. Even five minutes of physical activity a day can work wonders compared to none. While it is not a necessity for our spiritual lives, taking care of our bodies is a necessity for our physical lives. God made us both physical and spiritual, and we should strive to take care of both. When taking care of your body, there are four things you should focus on:

1. Intake
2. Exercise
3. Meditation
4. Looking good

Intake

Intake is what we put inside our bodies. There are certain things our bodies need in order to function properly. The most obvious thing we should intake is water. Our bodies are made mostly of water. We can survive weeks without food, but we will die after a few days without water. Water is the number one thing we need to keep our temples in tip-top shape.

Water keeps us looking young. It keeps the blood flowing and helps us digest food. It keeps toxins out of our bodies. Water is the wonder nectar of life. We should be well hydrated at all times. Clear urine is an indicator of being hydrated. There are different reports out there on how much water we should drink daily. I have heard a range of reports from 1 to 6 liters. Generally speaking, we should drink as much water as we can.

Personally, I aim for at least 1 to 3 liters per day; 6 liters is a lot of water. We can all start with 1 liter. Try to drink 1 liter per day, then work your way up. In order to drink more water, you may have to cut out some of your other drinks. This, however, will be well worth it. Drinking water in the morning can boost your immune system and wake your body up. Drinking water before a meal will help with digestion.

Fruits and vegetables should be eaten every day. Fruits and veggies provide us with a number of nutrients we need. At one point in my life, I was a carnivore; all I ate was meat, meat, and more meat. Now, I still enjoy eating meat, but I incorporate fruits and vegetables as well. If you don't have fruits and vegetables as an everyday part of your diet, your body will be malnourished. Eat fruit with your breakfast and lunch, and remember your greens.

Add supplements to your diet. Sometimes we can get really busy. We are always on the go. Supplements are helpful in times like this. Perhaps our eating habits have been off for the last few days. Supplements can keep us going. Vitamin C is very helpful for our immune system. A doctor suggested that I take a vitamin C pill once in the morning and once before going to bed. Ever since then, I have been doing that with a multivitamin. It is important to remember that taking vitamins is not a replacement for eating healthy. It is in addition to; it supplements the food we eat.

Knowing what not to put into our bodies can be just as important as knowing what to put. This is something you can decide for yourself personally. Just be smart and remember moderation. I know fried chicken is delicious, but try not to overdo it. Also, remember that just because something—whether it is a type of food, drug, or alcohol—is legal does not mean it is a good idea. Many people have become hooked on legal drugs. It is not shocking that people have even died as a result of legalized drugs. Being legal does not necessarily give you the green light. This is summed up in the verse below.

I Corinthians 6:12 – *"All things are lawful for me," but not all things are helpful. "All things are lawful for me," but I will not be dominated by anything.*

Exercise

We all know that we should do some exercise; yet, many of us do not. There are many reasons why we do not exercise. Some of us are too exhausted from work. Some of us do not want to spend our money on a gym membership, and some of us are just plain lazy. At some point in my life, I have been guilty of all of these. Exercising was much easier when I played football. In fact, it was mandatory. So, throughout high school and college and a few years afterwards, I was in great shape. It was a part of my everyday life.

However, once I started working, it became hard to find the time and energy to exercise. I know many of you out there can relate to that. We go on exercise binges before losing momentum, just like we do with our diets. But one realization helped me turn exercising back into an everyday part of my life—what I am exercising for now is different from what I was exercising for back then.

You see, I was exercising like I was still playing football. I realized, though, that I didn't need to lift weights like a football player or bodybuilder anymore. I was exercising simply to stay toned and healthy; that exercise is much different. You do not have to spend hours in the gym or run five miles a day in order to stay healthy. If you do, then that is great; keep it up. The reality for many of us, however, is that we do not have the time or desire to do that. That is why we lose momentum so easily.

The thing to remember is that doing a little exercise is better than doing nothing at all. Start off light and build momentum—or keep it light. If you can, go for a five-minute jog sandwiched between five minutes of walking. You can even start with just power walking. Then, work out a body section each day. One day, work out your arms, the next day your back, then legs, and so on. If you need time, go to sleep 20 minutes earlier and wake up 30 minutes earlier. Go for that light run in the morning right after you take your morning supplement. When you finish, come in, eat your breakfast, shower, and meditate to get your day started right.

Meditation

Meditation is a bit underrated, especially because it is compared with prayer. Many people pray, but far fewer people meditate. Meditation is talked about throughout the Bible. It can be of great benefit to us. Look at what the following verses say:

Psalm 143:5 – *I remember the days of old; I meditate on all that you have done; I ponder the work of your hands.*

Joshua 1:8 – *This Book of the Law shall not depart from your mouth, but you shall meditate on it day and night, so that you may be careful to do according to all that is written in it. For then you will make your way prosperous, and then you will have good success.*

Meditation is reflection. It is thinking on and contemplating something. You can meditate on reducing and relieving your stress, on having a good day, and on completing the task ahead of you. You can meditate on being a blessing to someone today. Meditation helps bring focus to you. It is also great for your physical health. As mentioned earlier, your physical and mental health can boost each other. Meditation plays a part in reducing stress and anxiety, which, in turn, may help reduce your chances of getting certain diseases.

Meditation should not be overlooked. Like exercising, you don't have to spend a long time meditating. Meditate for a few minutes when you wake up and right before you sleep. You can also meditate right before undertaking a task. That will help put you in the right mindset for the task. Many athletes from the high school to the professional level will meditate on their performances. We called this visualizing or doing mental reps. You will be surprised by the positive effect that visualization and meditation will have on you.

Looking Good

We used to have a saying in sports: if you look good, you play good. This is something I truly believe. I tell my students to dress better than normal when giving a presentation. Looking nice can increase your confidence. If you aspire to reach a certain position, dress as if you are already in that position. Fixing yourself up will make you feel better. This added confidence can lead you to performing better at a task.

Find your inner and outer beauty. Inner beauty has been known to make people more physically desirable. Find a style that you like and go with that. Learn to smile often. Smiling is the simplest way to immediately improve yourself. When the situation calls for it, dress yourself well. Everyone has the potential to look nice. Every human being has a natural beauty to them. Beauty comes in all shapes, sizes, heights, colors, hairstyles, and so on. We are all God's children. God made you well. Take pride in your appearance and make your temple look nice.

Genesis 1:31 - *And God saw everything that he had made, and behold, it was very good. And there was evening and there was morning, the sixth day.*

Ecclesiastes 9:8 - *Let your garments be always white. Let not oil be lacking on your head.*

Our lives and our bodies are gifts given to us by God. We should cherish, respect, and maintain our temples accordingly. While we cannot prevent every illness or mishap, we can still strive to maintain a healthy life. We never know what God may have in store for us in the future.

Jeremiah 29:11 – *For I know the plans I have for you, declares the Lord, plans for welfare and not for evil, to give you a future and a hope.*

Here is a recap of the tips/suggestions for maintaining a healthy life so we can increase our chances of living to a blessed, ripe old age.

1. Drink at least 1–3 liters of water per day.
2. Take a daily multivitamin to supplement your diet.
3. Incorporate fruits and vegetables into your diet.
4. Do some form of exercise at least 2–3 days per week. Something is better than nothing.
5. Meditate in the morning, at night, and before undertaking important tasks.
6. Be careful what you put into your body.
7. Remember moderation.
8. Make your temple look presentable.

4 MANAGE YOUR TIME

Ephesians 5:15-16 – *Look carefully then how you walk, not as unwise but as wise, making the best use of the time, because the days are evil.*

Sometimes we have conversations that change our lives. I had one of these conversations when I had the opportunity to learn from an extremely successful businessman. He asked me which was more valuable—time or money. He told me the answer was time; time is more valuable than money. You cannot make or enjoy money without time. Your time is a treasure. When you realize this, you will realize the importance of managing your time.

Proverbs 21:5 – *The plans of the diligent lead surely to abundance, but everyone who is hasty comes only to poverty.*

This short but crucial chapter is about time management. Time management is the planning of your time. It is making the best use of your time. Maximizing your time is a very powerful tool. It is impossible to be successful without managing your time. The difference between managing your time and not managing your time is astronomical. I cannot stress this enough. You will be surprised with the increase in your productivity when you start managing your time well. If you fail to plan, then you plan to fail.

Luke 14:28-30 – For which of you, desiring to build a tower, does not first sit down and count the cost, whether he has enough to complete it? Otherwise, when he has laid a foundation and is not able to finish, all who see it begin to mock him, saying, "This man began to build and was not able to finish."

Making various lists will help you manage your time. These lists consist of things you need to do—your to-do list. You can make a monthly, weekly, and daily to-do list. Use a calendar to keep track of your appointments, due dates, and other affairs. The monthly and weekly lists can be kept in your calendar. Make sure you check your calendar regularly, even daily. Each morning, you can make a list of the things you need to do that day. Alternatively, at night, you can list what needs to be done the next day. Actually write these lists out; do not try to keep them in your head. Your daily list should include items that will help you complete your weekly list. Your weekly list should have items that will help you to complete your monthly list. After you complete a task, cross it off of your list. This will allow you to see your progress—or lack thereof.

Psalm 90:12 – So teach us to number our days that we may get a heart of wisdom.

Making lists can help chunk your project and tasks. Chunking is breaking a task down into smaller, more manageable parts. You look to complete the first part of the task. When you are finished, you can go on to the next part. Always look toward the next step. If you break a task down like this, it will make it much more manageable. They say you eat an elephant one bite at a time. You also complete your goal one step at a time. That, in essence, is what chunking is. Chunking will prevent you from getting bogged down.

Momentum is lost when we start feeling bogged down. This leads to procrastination. We become weary and put our tasks off until later. Distractions start to become more appealing. We want to take a time-out to eat, watch

TV, and surf the Internet. We intend to do this only for a quick break; however, that quick break quickly turns into an hour—then two. The next thing we know, our whole day has been wasted. The flesh is weak, lazy, and does not like to work. That is why we have to discipline ourselves. We must work to eliminate these distractions.

I Corinthians 9:26-27 – *So I do not run aimlessly; I do not box as one beating the air. But I discipline my body and keep it under control, lest after preaching to others I myself should be disqualified.*

Hebrews 6:11-12 – *And we desire each one of you to show the same earnestness to have the full assurance of hope until the end, so that you may not be sluggish, but imitators of those who through faith and patience inherit the promises.*

Learn to prioritize. Some things are simply more important than others. When you make your lists, especially your daily list, rank the tasks by importance. Complete the most important task first. When you are finished with that one, then move on to the next one. Do this until your list is complete. One piece of advice that I often hear is, do not make checking your email the first thing you do in the morning. Email can easily become one of those distractions that can lead to procrastination.

Jesus suggested that we prioritize. He directed us to seek the kingdom of God first. That is telling us to do the most important thing first; in this case, it is seeking the kingdom of God. We can take that and apply it to other aspects of our lives. Instead of always wanting to have fun and be entertained, do your work first. Let everyone else play while you get better. Keep your eyes on the prize.

Matthew 6:33 – *But seek first the kingdom of God and his righteousness, and all these things will be added to you.*

I Peter 4:3-4 – *For the time that is past suffices for doing what the Gentiles want to do, living in sensuality, passions, drunkenness, orgies, drinking parties, and lawless idolatry. With respect to this they are surprised when you do not join them in the same flood of debauchery, and they malign you*

Philippians 3:14 – *I press on toward the goal for the prize of the upward call of God in Christ Jesus.*

Alan Lakein, a famous time management author, said that time equals life. Therefore, if you waste your time, you waste your life. This is true. This is also why time is more valuable than money. In order to get the most out of your life, you need to get the most out of your time. This separates the average from the great. Your time is precious. Do not waste it. Make the most of every opportunity.

Colossians 4:5 – Walk in wisdom toward outsiders, making the best use of the time.

To be clear, I think enjoyment is an important and necessary part of your life; it is just not always the most important part. This is why you prioritize and manage your time. Keep in mind that you work for a reason. The reason is so that you can make a living, provide for your family, and afford to enjoy your life. As a matter of fact, taking vacations and making time to relax will recharge you, thereby allowing you to work more efficiently. So, when making your lists, reward your hard work by factoring in some time for rest and relaxation. There is a time for everything. This includes fun.

Ecclesiastes 3:1 – For everything there is a season, and a time for every matter under heaven

Ecclesiastes 5:18 – Behold, what I have seen to be good and fitting is to eat and drink and find enjoyment in all the toil with which one toils under the sun the few days of his life that God has given him, for this is his lot.

5 EAT, DRINK AND BE MERRY

Ecclesiastes 8:15 – And I commend joy, for man has nothing better under the sun but to eat and drink and be joyful, for this will go with him in his toil through the days of his life that God has given him under the sun.

Many religions are built around the idea of eternal life. The goal is to live in a way that puts us in God's favor. We dream of enjoying heaven, speaking with biblical heroes, reuniting with our loved ones, and walking the streets of gold. This is all well and good, but it is far from the only thing.

We often forget about this life. Our only focus is on the afterlife. We make rules in order to help us reach salvation. However, the rules can easily lead to a restricted life drained of enjoyment. Instead of being friendly with each other, we look at other people's lives and judge them based upon the personal rules that we have laid out for ourselves. Rules are definitely needed; but it is important to remember that rules are made to keep order, not to be blindly followed. The Pharisees tried to judge Jesus based on rules that were mostly man's tradition. The Jews were not supposed to work on the Sabbath. However, Jesus had to remind them that we are not made to blindly follow rules. Rules are made to benefit us. They are not made to box us in to a restricted life. If a rule does not benefit the people, perhaps it needs to be reconsidered.

Mark 2:24-27 – And the Pharisees were saying to him, "Look, why are they doing what is not lawful on the Sabbath?" And he said to them, "Have you never read what David did, when he was in need and was hungry, he and those who were with him: how he entered the house of God, in the time of Abiathar the high priest, and ate the bread of the Presence, which it is not lawful for any but the priests to eat, and also gave it to those who were with him?" And he said to them, "The Sabbath was made for man, not man for the Sabbath.

Mark 3:4-5 – And he said to them, "Is it lawful on the Sabbath to do good or to do harm, to save life or to kill?" But they were silent. And he looked around at them with anger, grieved at their hardness of heart, and said to the man, "Stretch out your hand." He stretched it out, and his hand was restored.

God did not create us to be robots and automatons. He gave us this life here on Earth. Life is a gift from God and we should enjoy our time on Earth.

Ecclesiastes 2:24 – There is nothing better for a person than that he should eat and drink and find enjoyment in his toil. This also, I saw, is from the hand of God.

God wants us to be happy in this life. Take a look at Psalm 100 below. This is a happy chapter; I imagine that the author was having a great day when he wrote it.

Psalm 100 – Make a joyful noise to the Lord, all the earth! Serve the Lord with gladness! Come into his presence with singing! Know that the Lord, he is God! It is he who made us, and we are his; we are his people, and the sheep of his pasture. Enter his gates with thanksgiving, and his courts with praise! Give thanks to him; bless his name! For the Lord is good; his steadfast love endures forever, and his faithfulness to all generations.

There is no iota of sadness or anger in that chapter. Sadness and anger are negative emotions that lead to negative behaviors. If we do not correct them, the negatives will add up, break us down, and prevent us from having the life we deserve—one that is happy, peaceful, and filled with joy.

Proverbs 15:13 – *A glad heart makes a cheerful face, but by sorrow of heart the spirit is crushed.*

Proverbs 17:22 – *A joyful heart is good medicine, but a crushed spirit dries up the bones.*

Galatians 5:22-23 – *But the fruit of the Spirit is love, joy, peace, patience, kindness, goodness, faithfulness, gentleness, self-control; against such things there is no law.*

Luke 24:36 – *As they were talking about these things, Jesus himself stood among them, and said to them, "Peace to you!"*

While there are times when we will have sorrow in our lives, we should not be dominated by it. We all have stress factors. Solomon wrote about this feeling and even Jesus became sad, frustrated, and upset at times.

Ecclesiastes 2:17 – *So I hated life, because what is done under the sun was grievous to me, for all is vanity and a striving after wind.*

Mark 11:15 – *And they came to Jerusalem. And he (Jesus) entered the temple and began to drive out those who sold and those who bought in the temple, and he overturned the tables of the money-changers and the seats of those who sold pigeons.*

John 11:35 – *Jesus wept.*

Too many of us are stressed on a regular basis. That should not be. Stress can be caused by a number of factors, including our relationships with our friends and family, bills, lack of drive and motivation, lack of hope, our jobs, and more. To directly pinpoint the source of stress—it comes from worrying about these problems. Some of us let these problems cause us to be anxious. Our mind is constantly on them. In football, we used to have a motto: Take things one game at a time, one day at a time, and one play at a time. Being overanxious can cause us to overlook something or perform halfheartedly. We need to stay in the present and not let our minds wander.

Matthew 6:34 – *"Therefore do not be anxious about tomorrow, for tomorrow will be anxious for itself. Sufficient for the day is its own trouble..."*

I Peter 5:7 – *cast all your anxieties on him, because he cares for you.*

Philippians 4:6-7 – *do not be anxious about anything, but in everything by prayer and supplication with thanksgiving let your requests be made known to God. And the peace of God, which surpasses all understanding, will guard your hearts and your minds in Christ Jesus.*

We worry because we are scared of an unwanted outcome becoming real. We see the possibility of a situation becoming negative. This is something we should overcome. It is important to realize that worrying does absolutely nothing but make us sick. Worrying does not solve the problem—only prayer and action do that. Have faith that with prayer, action, and a plan, you will solve the problem. Do as much as you can to remedy the situation and let God do the rest.

We must decide decisively not to be fearful. If we do what we need to, things will be okay. Everything will not go exactly how we want, but trust that God knows what he is doing. Do not fear. We are not intended to be fearful creatures. We are supposed to have a sound mind.

II Timothy 1:7 – *for God gave us a spirit not of fear but of power and love and self-control.*

Psalm 91:5 – *You will not fear the terror of the night, nor the arrow that flies by day,*

Psalm 4:8 – *In peace I will both lie down and sleep; for you alone, O Lord, make me dwell in safety.*

Mark 5:36 – *But overhearing what they said, Jesus said to the ruler of the synagogue, "Do not fear, only believe."*

We should expect to be prosperous. Some of us do not believe that we will ever truly be prosperous. We rationalize our poverty as a type of virtuous righteousness. Some of us view our situation as a type of self-penance and do not believe that we deserve to be prosperous. We believe that having money will cause us to become corrupt. To this I say, have a little faith in yourself and in God. We are not supposed to be poor. We do not need to be Bill Gates rich, but we should be able to pay our bills and enjoy life. Becoming prosperous is not easy, but it is something God will bless us with and provide.

Philippians 4:19 – And my God will supply every need of yours according to his riches in glory in Christ Jesus.

Luke 11:10 –For everyone who asks receives, and the one who seeks finds, and to the one who knocks it will be opened.

Psalm 37:25 – I have been young, and now am old, yet I have not seen the righteous forsaken or his children begging for bread.

God also puts people in our lives that provide for us emotionally. These people are our friends and family. In the bible, Jonathan and David were best friends, Jesus had his disciples, and Paul's letters were sent to people whom he called friends. Friends make life more colorful and enjoyable. We should enjoy our time with our friends and family.

Psalm 133:1 – *Behold, how good and pleasant it is when brothers dwell in unity!*

Proverbs 17:17 – *A friend loves at all times, and a brother is born for adversity.*

We were all children at one time. Children have an innocent, positive outlook on life. They have big dreams that they believe they can accomplish and they are excited about life. It is not until the world and its many problems are thrust upon us that we become more stressed and pessimistic. If you look at people who always seem happy and excited, you will notice that they keep their inner child alive. We all have our inner child. If you find a way to keep him/her alive, it will make your life much merrier. This does not mean being childish or shirking your responsibility. Rather, have a lively, optimistic excitement about life. Life is always presenting us with new situations and people. Embrace this.

Matthew 18:4 – *Whoever humbles himself like this child is the greatest in the kingdom of heaven.*

We should expect to be happy. The world can be a rough place, but we deserve to live a merry life. We often forget that this life is precious. God gives us this one earthen life. Make the most of it. Enjoy it. Enjoy the people and things God has put in your life. Eat, drink, and be merry. If you ask, God will make this life a happy and joyous one.

John 16:24 – *Until now you have asked nothing in my name. Ask, and you will receive, that your joy may be full.*

One way in which we can ensure that we have a merry life is by giving. Giving can make us happy. Have you ever given a gift to someone or given to a charity? Afterwards, you probably felt good inside. This is not selfish; it is okay to feel good about doing good. Giving and receiving is a cycle. If you make someone happy, you will be happy. So make giving a part of your life. It is a win-win.

6 GIVE AND IT SHALL BE GIVEN

<u>Luke 6:38</u> – Give, and it will be given to you. Good measure, pressed down, shaken together, running over, will be put into your lap. For with the measure you use it will be measured back to you.

Every year, the day after Thanksgiving (better known as Black Friday) kicks off the Christmas season. This is when people start to kick their Christmas shopping, planning, and decorating into high gear. It is sometimes called a magical time and is referred to as the most wonderful time of the year.

This time is considered wonderful because the principle of giving and receiving is in full effect. Giving and receiving plays a huge part in improving our lives. It is essential. Giving, like money, is a medium of exchange. It is a currency. Money is used to get something you want. Giving, too, gives us something we want; something we need!

If you take a look at many successful people, you will find that, oftentimes, they have learned the principle of giving. They may even be considered jerks in other regards, but they have learned the law of giving. Bill Gates, Warren Buffett, and Peyton Manning are three examples of men whom I respect and of whom I consider myself a fan. These men have mastered the principle of giving. It is no surprise that they are very successful.

Both Bill Gates and Warren Buffett have two of the world's largest charitable organizations. Gates started the Bill & Melinda Gates Foundation and Buffett started the Buffett Foundation. Gates and Buffett signed a pledge together, promising that they would give away at least fifty percent of their wealth. In fact, both men have stated that they would like to give away more than ninety percent of their wealth.

Peyton Manning is one of my all-time favorite NFL quarterbacks. It is not just his stellar play and computer-like calculations on the gridiron that are impressive; the fact that he gives back off the field is also notable. He has started his own foundation—the Peyback Foundation—that helps disadvantaged kids. In an effort to honor his contributions, the St. Vincent Hospital in Indianapolis renamed its children's wing after him. It is said that Manning would anonymously visit the children there—no press, no cameras. He wanted to make it about the children, not about him.

Giving should be a regular part of our lives. God loves and honors this. The more you give, the more God will bless you. Blessings should flow in and out of our lives. I pray that God blesses me so that I can, in turn, bless others. The more blessings you sow, the more blessings you will reap.

Luke 6:31 – And as you wish that others would do to you, do so to them.

Proverbs 11:25 – Whoever brings blessing will be enriched, and one who waters will himself be watered.

Most people do not have Bill Gates, Warren Buffett, or Peyton Manning money. That is alright. You can give according to what you have or what your heart tells you. Jesus and his disciples took notice of those giving in the temple. Some people were giving decent amounts of money. However, Jesus said it was the woman who gave the two pennies who had given the most. This is because she gave all that she had. Giving is not a competition. Give what God has blessed you to give.

Luke 21:1-4 – Jesus looked up and saw the rich putting their gifts into the offering box, and he saw a poor widow put in two small copper coins. And he said, "Truly, I tell you, this poor widow has put in more than all of them. For they all contributed out of their abundance, but she out of her poverty put in all she had to live on."

There are also ways to give that don't involve money. Our time is a valuable thing that we can give away. We can volunteer at a local charity. We can help out at our church or at a school event. Find your strength and help people in that area. If you are good at math, do some tutoring. You can also blog your expert advice. Send out a weekly or monthly email of encouragement. You can give in countless ways. Use your strengths and be creative with them. Have fun giving. God loves a cheerful giver.

II Corinthians 9:7 – Each one must give as he has decided in his heart, not reluctantly or under compulsion, for God loves a cheerful giver.

Acts 20:35 – In all things I have shown you that by working hard in this way we must help the weak and remember the words of the Lord Jesus, how he himself said, "It is more blessed to give than to receive."

Giving is great, but it often overshadows receiving. We internalize that giving is better than receiving. This is true as far as attitude is concerned. Our thoughts and attitude should be about giving joy to others, not just receiving joy. However, if we have the right intentions, receiving can be just as powerful as giving. We often forget the receiving part of the currency. You cannot give without someone receiving.

One of the most important lessons I learned while teaching in China was that I should receive gracefully. Generous hospitality toward, and treatment of, one's guests is a very important part of Chinese culture. However, this contrasted with my attitude. When people would offer to do something for me, I would respond by saying, "Oh you don't have to do that. I appreciate it though." I believe this was a part of my Western culture. I thought I was doing them a favor by turning them down. However, I would notice that whenever I said that, a look of disappointment would emerge on their faces. Instead of being polite and saving them time and money like I thought, I was actually robbing them of the joy of blessing someone.

You see, humans love to make other people happy. We get joy by bringing joy to others—and that is a great thing. I had to learn to receive gracefully. When I did this, I could see the happiness on their faces. They enjoyed bringing a smile to my face and I enjoyed bringing a smile to theirs. We were giving and receiving at the same time!

This is what Jesus was doing when he accepted Zacchaeus' dinner invitation. Zacchaeus was so happy to have Jesus come to his house that he pledged to give away half of his goods to the poor. Notice that it was Jesus receiving Zacchaeus that caused Zacchaeus to give some more. The currency continued because there was both cheerful giving and graceful receiving.

Luke 19:5-8 – And when Jesus came to the place, he looked up and said to him, "Zacchaeus, hurry and come down, for I must stay at your house today." So he hurried and came down and received him joyfully. And when they saw it, they all grumbled, "He has gone in to be the guest of a man who is a sinner." And Zacchaeus stood and said to the Lord, "Behold, Lord, the half of my goods I give to the poor. And if I have defrauded anyone of anything, I restore it fourfold."

Giving and receiving is a law. The Lion King called this the circle of life. It occurs all the time in nature. We breathe in oxygen that is given off by trees. The trees, in turn, receive carbon dioxide that we breathe out. This is a natural cycle of giving and receiving. Animals eat from the earth and, when they die, they feed the earth. The moon receives light from the sun, then turns around and lights up our night sky.

Just as giving and receiving happens in nature all the time, this principle should also be enacted in our lives all the time. When you give, do not just give in order to receive. Give because it is the natural and right thing to do. Give and receive to bring joy to others. Make giving fun. Think about ways you can happily give. Then give without expecting anything in return.

Luke 6:35 – But love your enemies, and do good, and lend, expecting nothing in return, and your reward will be great, and you will be sons of the Most High, for he is kind to the ungrateful and the evil.

This is the kind of giving that God loves and respects. Some people give for the accolades. They love it when people talk about how great they are. They like to be put on a pedestal. That is one reason why I am impressed with Peyton Manning. When he went on his hospital visits, he went anonymously. He made it about the people he was visiting. That is awesome and something we can emulate.

Matthew 6:2 – *Thus, when you give to the needy, sound no trumpet before you, as the hypocrites do in the synagogues and in the streets, that they may be praised by others. Truly, I say to you, they have received their reward.*

For a long time, I did not understand the power of giving. I reasoned that if I was always giving, then I would be losing money, time, etc. However, and fortunately, it does not work like that. Giving opens us up for more things in our lives. This is why if we give, then it will be given unto us. We are made to be giving creatures. Make giving and receiving a part of your daily life. Keep the currency, the love, and the blessings flowing in and out of your life. Giving is a part of charity and love. We have faith, we have hope, and we have love. The greatest of these is love.

I Corinthians 13:13 – *So now faith, hope, and love abide, these three; but the greatest of these is love.*

7 MONEY ANSWERS ALL THINGS

I Timothy 6:10 – *For the love of money is a root of all kinds of evils. It is through this craving that some have wandered away from the faith and pierced themselves with many pangs.*

If you ask someone what the Bible says about money, he/she will often misquote the above verse, saying that money is the root of all evil. However, the verse actually says that it is the "love of money" that is the root of all evil. Misquoting this verse gives us an irrational and detrimental view of money. The fact of the matter is that money is very important and necessary. We need money to buy food, take care of our family, pay for college, keep shelter over our head, etc. Money answers everything.

Ecclesiastes 10:19 – *Bread is made for laughter, and wine gladdens life, and money answers everything.*

Everyone knows that we need money. Pretending that wanting money is a bad thing can prevent us from flourishing. Even worse, it can give us a fear of money. If we fear money, then money controls us. It becomes our master. Instead, we need to learn about money, learn to have control over our finances, and be the master of money.

Matthew 6:24 – No one can serve two masters, for either he will hate the one and love the other, or he will be devoted to the one and despise the other. You cannot serve God and money.

The first part of being the master of our money is having the correct view of it. Money in the right hands is a great thing. The more money you have, the more you can be a blessing with it. Do not be afraid to make more money. Do not feel guilty about wanting more money. Someone has to make that money. It is preferable for it to be in the hands of good people than corrupt people. God may want you to use that money for something that is needed in the future. You may find a loved one needing an expensive operation that is not covered by insurance. It is possible that God may bless you with the money so that you can, in turn, be a blessing. Do not limit what God will do through you.

Money is a tool that can be used to make our lives enjoyable. However, like any other tool, it can be used incorrectly. It is your responsibility to learn about how to work with your money. You, and you alone, are responsible for making your financial situation better. Your parents, friends, teachers, accountant, or anyone else are not responsible for you. Read books on money. Become educated on how to handle it.

The first thing you must realize is that there is no such thing as free or easy money. Believe me, I have searched unsuccessfully for easy money. Whatever endeavor you undertake will require hard work, time, and effort. Listen to rich people talking about how they made their money. Unless they won the lottery or inherited wealth, they all put a great amount of work into their task. We can believe in ourselves and have all the faith we want; but if we are lazy and give minimum effort, then faith does not matter. Put in the work!

James 2:17 – So also faith by itself, if it does not have works, is dead

Proverbs 10:4 – A slack hand causes poverty, but the hand of the diligent makes rich.

It is important to put the principle of giving and receiving into action with our money. Money is currency—a means of exchange. Money is intended to be ever-flowing—coming in and going out. If we keep this cycle going, it only becomes stronger. The more we give, the more we will receive.

Proverbs 11:24 – *One gives freely, yet grows all the richer; another withholds what he should give, and only suffers want.*

There are many different outlets for giving. You can give to a church, give to a charity, or donate to a school or scholarship program. Your community will always need money. That is true no matter where you live. Be in the mindset of giving back when you can. Ask God to put something specific on your heart to donate to and support. You will find something that you will be excited about supporting. When you have discovered who you want to give to and the amount, you can give cheerfully. If you don't have the money to give yet, tell God you need more money in order to be a blessing.

Giving is much better than lending money. If you loan people money, they will feel obligated to pay you back. That could become a burden hanging over them, especially if they are not able to pay it back in a timely manner.

Relationships have been destroyed because of money. I have a friend who always warns against letting money ruin a friendship. The best way to ensure that money will not ruin a friendship is by not lending to friends. Do not lend money to your family either. If your friends or family do need money from you, give it to them. Tell them they can pay it back whenever they are able, but not to worry about it too much. After you tell them that, you should forget about it as well. If they pay you back, that is great. If not, that is okay too; it was a gift. Try not to put your loved ones in the position of being obligated to you.

Similarly, you should be careful about borrowing money too. This is not just from friends and family, but from any entity. There may be times that you may need to borrow money; just make sure it is your best option. Do your research, find out the interest rate, read the small print, and have a plan to pay it back. It is best not to owe anyone money. When you owe someone money, you are indebted to that person.

Proverbs 22:7 – The rich rules over the poor, and the borrower is the slave of the lender.

We can cut down on borrowing if we learn to live within our means. We are all guilty of trying to keep up with the Joneses at some point in time. This leads to us purchasing things we do not really need and cannot afford. Don't get me wrong—you should enjoy life and spend on yourself sometimes; just do not splurge to the point where it hurts you. Do not buy that new dress if your light bill is past due.

Our worth is not determined by how much money we have but by what we contribute. History is littered with people who were poor but contributed. It is easy to look at the TV and idolize celebrities. However, we fail to realize that we do not idolize them because of their money, but rather because of what they have contributed to our lives. Maybe a singer contributed a great song that seems to speak to you, or an athlete gives you a target to shoot for and try to accomplish. It is their contributions that matter—not their money. You do not need to be the richest person to be able to contribute. Therefore, it is not necessary to keep up with the Joneses. Live within your means and do not covet what other people have.

Luke 12:15 - *And he said to them, "Take care, and be on your guard against all covetousness, for one's life does not consist in the abundance of his possessions."*

Acts 20:33 – *I coveted no one's silver or gold or apparel.*

If you want to have more possessions, learn how to budget your money. There was a time in my life where I thought there was a hole in my bank account. I could not save any money. On paper, I was making enough to cover my bills and save a decent chunk of money, but that was simply not happening. This was because I was not keeping a budget of my money. After one of my friends presented me with a monthly budget plan, I was able to start saving.

You will be surprised how much more money you can save with a budget. Calculate your monthly expenses and keep track of everything you purchase. Create a budget sheet and adjust it to fit your expenses. Take away your monthly expenses—such as mortgage/rent, utilities, insurance, gas, food, loan payments, phone bill, miscellaneous—and subtract them from your net pay. With the money that is left over, set some aside for savings, retirement, and investments. It is both wise and necessary to keep track of what you have and what you spend.

Proverbs 27:23 – *Know well the condition of your flocks, and give attention to your herds*

Luke 16:10 – *One who is faithful in a very little is also faithful in much, and one who is dishonest in a very little is also dishonest in much.*

One thing you should save up for is a nest egg—money set aside for a rainy day. Unexpected expenses will arise. Problems will come. You might lose your job, your company could downsize, a natural disaster could strike, or your investments might go under. These things happen to the best of us; we must be prepared. If you are prepared for the unexpected, then it is not really unexpected. A nest egg is money set aside so you can survive for at least 3–6 months without a steady income if need be. Do not wait until it is too late to be prepared.

Proverbs 6:6-8 – Go to the ant, O sluggard; consider her ways, and be wise. Without having any chief, officer, or ruler, she prepares her bread in summer and gathers her food in harvest.

Speaking of being prepared, get insurance: car, life, health, and whatever else may be necessary. It might seem expensive and a waste of money, but it is great to have insurance on the occasions when you actually need it. The concept of the nest egg is the same—be prepared for the unexpected. Insurance, in theory, protects us from various dangers.

Proverbs 22:3 – The prudent sees danger and hides himself, but the simple go on and suffer for it.

Alongside a nest egg and insurance, contribute a portion of your income to your retirement. There are a few viable options—mutual funds, Roth IRA, 401K, etc. Have more than one of these if possible. Do not rely on social security as your retirement plan. Do not spend and devour all of your money on things that will gratify you now. Even if you have only a little to start with, start now. Prepare to enjoy the latter years with which God will bless you.

Proverbs 21:20 – Precious treasure and oil are in a wise man's dwelling, but a foolish man devours it.

Remember to pay Uncle Sam. We are required to pay our taxes. Many people do not like taxes. I understand that; but no organization, church, fraternity, or country can run without money. Taxes (in theory) go to the continued development of one's country. Find a book, accountant, friend, etc. to learn what you are required to pay. If you are justifiably required to pay the tax, then pay the tax and avoid an audit nightmare. You will be glad you did.

Mark 12:17 – Jesus said to them, "Render to Caesar the things that are Caesar's, and to God the things that are God's." And they marveled at him.

Money is an everyday part of life. So is death. No matter how invincible or Superman-like I feel sometimes, I know one day I will leave this life. I also know I cannot take my money with me. It has to go somewhere. This is where a will comes in handy. A will distributes your wealth and assets to where you want them to go when you pass. You can spread it out amongst your family, donate it to a charity or organization, have a combination of both, or do something else with it. Warren Buffet has stated that he will give his children some of his wealth but give most of it to charity. You can even start giving it away while you are alive. No matter what you decide, make sure you have a will.

Proverbs 13:22 – *A good man leaves an inheritance to his children's children...*

Money is like a game, job, or sport. At first, dealing with money and the different expenditures can seem complicated and daunting. However, the more familiar and educated we become, the easier and more natural our dealings will become. Have a plan for your money. Research and implement the suggestions laid out here. Money is a gift from God. Do good deeds with your money. Own your money; control your money; build your money

8 LET HE WHO IS WITHOUT SIN

Spirituality is mankind's attempt to move closer to God. It is us trying to get on God's page and become one with him. This was Jesus' prayer.

John 17:20-21 – _"I do not ask for these only, but also for those who will believe in me through their word, that they may all be one, just as you, Father, are in me, and I in you, that they also may be in us, so that the world may believe that you have sent me…"_

However, sometimes we seem to forget our mission and goal. Some of us seem to live to be "holier than thou." This has caused a perception (or misconception) that equates religion with being judgmental bigots instead of being about the good news. Gossip has become synonymous with the church. Religious leaders come across as angry and full of hate instead of full of love.

Sometimes, I wonder if these outspoken people read the Bible to improve their lives and this world, or if they try to use it for the purpose of justifying their actions.

If our goal is to be like Jesus, let us see what Jesus did and said. If Jesus were alive today, many of the religious would treat him the way they did 2,000 years ago. They looked down on Jesus, calling him a gluttonous alcoholic who hangs out with sinners. The Pharisees (religious leaders at that time) even called Jesus a liar and tried to stone him.

Luke 7:34 – The Son of Man has come eating and drinking, and you say, "Look at him! A glutton and a drunkard, a friend of tax collectors and sinners!"

Luke 19:7 – And when they saw it, they all grumbled, "He has gone in to be the guest of a man who is a sinner."

John 8:13 – So the Pharisees said to him, "You are bearing witness about yourself; your testimony is not true."

John 8:59 – So they picked up stones to throw at him, but Jesus hid himself and went out of the temple.

When questioned about why he hung out with and spent time around sinners, look at Jesus' response:

Matthew 9:11-13 – And when the Pharisees saw this, they said to his disciples, "Why does your teacher eat with tax collectors and sinners?" But when he heard it, he said, "Those who are well have no need of a physician, but those who are sick. Go and learn what this means, 'I desire mercy, and not sacrifice.' For I came not to call the righteous, but sinners."

It is those that are struggling who need our help, in the same way that it is the sick who need a doctor. You cannot tell people about the good news if you never talk to them and are never around. More time should be spent interacting and less time judging. The title of this chapter is "Let He Who is Without Sin..." Let us take a look at the powerful story that is the source of these words:

John 8:1-11 – but Jesus went to the Mount of Olives. Early in the morning he came again to the temple. All the people came to him, and he sat down and taught them. The scribes and the Pharisees brought a woman who had been caught in adultery, and placing her in the midst they said to him, "Teacher, this woman has been caught in the act of adultery. Now in the Law Moses commanded us to stone such women. So what do you say?" This they said to test him, that they might have some charge to bring against him. Jesus bent down and wrote with his finger on the ground. And as they continued to ask him, he stood up and said to them, "Let him who is without sin among you be the first to throw a stone at her." And once more he bent down and wrote on the ground. But when they heard it, they went away one by one, beginning with the older ones, and Jesus was left alone with the woman standing before him. Jesus stood up and said to her, "Woman, where are they? Has no one condemned you?" She said, "No one, Lord." And Jesus said, "Neither do I condemn you; go, and from now on sin no more."

The religious had judged this woman to be a sinner—and rightfully so. She was caught in the act. However, instead of condemning her, Jesus said that whoever was without sin should throw the first stone. No one could throw the first stone. That is because everyone has sinned. Everyone has made mistakes.

Romans 3:23 – for all have sinned and fall short of the glory of God

Since we have all sinned, we all need to be forgiven. We should keep that in mind when others need our forgiveness. Jesus encourages us to forgive rather than condemn.

Matthew 6:14 – For if you forgive others their trespasses, your heavenly Father will also forgive you

Matthew 18:21-22 – Then Peter came up and said to him, "Lord, how often will my brother sin against me, and I forgive him? As many as seven times?" Jesus said to him, "I do not say to you seven times, but seventy times seven..."

You cannot forgive if you are constantly judging and trying to live "holier than thou." The Pharisees condemned and judged. Jesus interacted and forgave. We should try to be more Christ-like instead of Pharisee-like. The way some so-called religious leaders act toward women, gays, and other minority groups is downright appalling. I have heard religious leaders make the statement that "God hates fags." For one, that is not true. Also, think about that. Is that kind of talk Godlike? Does that sound like righteous speak? Is that the type of person God wants to hang out with in Heaven? Is that speech going to make people want to read the Bible?

Even the in-fighting amongst "believers" is, at times, absurd. Much of the discord comes because we have not learned our jobs. We have not discovered how God wants to use us. Each of us has a job to do—a special way we can contribute to the world.

Ephesians 4:11-12 – And he gave the apostles, the prophets, the evangelists, the shepherds and teachers, to equip the saints for the work of ministry, for building up the body of Christ

The problem is that we do not know our calling. Too many people try to act like pastors. Pastors try to do the job of evangelists. People try to pastor people who are not a part of their church. This is not to say that we cannot hold each other accountable. However, there is a difference between judging and holding someone accountable. First, you hold your brother and sister accountable—that is, the people who share a similar belief. If two people are trying to lose weight together, they can hold each other accountable. But if I am not on a diet and not trying to lose weight, they cannot hold me accountable the same way they hold each other accountable. This is because I am on a different page. This also applies to holding others spiritually accountable—you need to be on the same page first.

Furthermore, holding someone accountable comes from love. Judging comes from hate. You may truly be meaning to do well, but it is still hate. Deep down, you know which one you are coming from. Some people try to justify their feelings by saying that they hate the sin, not the sinner. That line is often a cop-out. Your fruit, or what comes from you, bears witness to you.

Matthew 7:16 – _You will recognize them by their fruits._

Your fruit will tell on you. It will show if you are coming from love or hate. Does your demeanor, speech, and actions reflect a righteous, loving manner toward those who do not believe what you believe? Are you really being accountable or are you judging?

Matthew 7:1-5 – *"Judge not, that you be not judged. For with the judgment you pronounce you will be judged, and with the measure you use it will be measured to you. Why do you see the speck that is in your brother's eye, but do not notice the log that is in your own eye? Or how can you say to your brother, 'Let me take the speck out of your eye,' when there is the log in your own eye? You hypocrite, first take the log out of your own eye, and then you will see clearly to take the speck out of your brother's eye..."*

Jesus says not to judge. He then suggests that if you are judging, maybe you should reevaluate where you are coming from. Think about how the people to whom you are "witnessing" will perceive your speech. Think about how you treat those who do not believe what you believe.

Luke 6:27-37 – *"But I say to you who hear, Love your enemies, do good to those who hate you, bless those who curse you, pray for those who abuse you. To one who strikes you on the cheek, offer the other also, and from one who takes away your cloak do not withhold your tunic either. Give to everyone who begs from you, and from one who takes away your goods do not demand them back. And as you wish that others would do to you, do so to them. 'If you love those who love you, what benefit is that to you? For even sinners love those who love them. And if you do good to those who do good to you, what benefit is that to you? For even sinners do the same. And if you lend to those from whom you expect to receive, what credit is that to you? Even sinners lend to sinners, to get back the same amount. But love your enemies, and do good, and lend, expecting nothing in return, and your reward will be great, and you will be sons of the Most High, for he is kind to the ungrateful and the evil. Be merciful, even as your Father is merciful.' Judge not, and you will not be judged; condemn not, and you will not be condemned; forgive, and you will be forgiven..."*

We all need mercy at some point. Mistakes will be made and sins will occur. We should learn from our mistakes in order to make us better and to ensure that they don't keep us down. A just man knows that when he falls, he can get back up. When you fall, do not stay down. Get back up and get back on track. By the same token, when others are down, do not judge them. Do not kick them when they are down. Do not be crabs in a bucket—do not pull each other down; help each other up. That is the loving, righteous, Christ-like thing to do.

Proverbs 24:16-17 – *for the righteous falls seven times and rises again, but the wicked stumble in times of calamity. Do not rejoice when your enemy falls, and let not your heart be glad when he stumbles,*

The name of the game here is love. Love is the greatest human need. Research has shown that babies need human touch (what they perceive as love). Touch is linked to babies growing healthily; it prevents certain illnesses from developing. Love—at least, the perception of love—is required for survival. It is the feeling of no love that has caused certain people to give up on their lives.

People are looking to be led by love. People can also read through phoniness. If we do not have love, what we say or do does not matter. It will be perceived as being judgmental and compassionless. To have passion is a great thing. However, do not be passionate about what you hate. Be passionate about what you love. Love combined with passion will yield compassion. You can be that example of love to the world.

Galatians 6:10 – *So then, as we have opportunity, let us do good to everyone, and especially to those who are of the household of faith.*

I Corinthians 13:1 – *If I speak in the tongues of men and of angels, but have not love, I am a noisy gong or a clanging cymbal.*

This world is in need of more love. Too many people are depressed. Too many people are being killed. Too many people are giving up on life. Jesus came to this world out of his love for mankind. He operated out of love. You, too, should operate out of love. You can make the world better if you operate in and through love. After all, this is your true nature. You were made in the image of God, and God is love. Therefore, you, too, are love. Let your light shine in a way that exudes love.

John 3:16-17 – *"For God so loved the world, that he gave his only Son, that whoever believes in him should not perish but have eternal life. For God did not send his Son into the world to condemn the world, but in order that the world might be saved through him..."*

I John 3:16-18 – *By this we know love, that he laid down his life for us, and we ought to lay down our lives for the brothers. But if anyone has the world's goods and sees his brother in need, yet closes his heart against him, how does God's love abide in him? Little children, let us not love in word or talk but in deed and in truth.*

9 LET YOUR LIGHT SHINE

Matthew 5:16 – *In the same way, let your light shine before others, so that they may see your good works and give glory to your Father who is in heaven.*

To let your light shine means to be an example. People are always looking for someone to look up to and admire. Oftentimes, people look up to athletes, musicians, actors, and other celebrities. Sometimes, it is even the undesirables—the drug dealers and gang members—who are admired. However, there are two ways in which we can be the example that people are seeking. We set an example through our tasks as well as through our character.

Tasks

We all have tasks and goals we want to accomplish. People need to believe if they want to accomplish their goals. To some people, those attainable goals seem out of reach; but you give people hope when you succeed. By accomplishing your goals and completing your tasks, you become living proof that it can be done.

Those goals that you accomplish, no matter how insignificant they may seem, could lead to something great for mankind. What if George Washington or Martin Luther King Jr. decided to live quiet, normal lives? What if the Wright brothers did not invent the airplane? What if the creator of ice cream never invented it? These are examples of people who contributed significantly to mankind. Many unknown people have contributed to mankind. God gave us all something special to contribute; it is a matter of whether or not we are willing to make the effort to do so.

God gave us all gifts; but we must discover that gift and use it. Many people not only waste their gift; they fail to even discover what their gift is. Your gift may be singing, coaching, teaching, being a great manager or employee, writing a book or movie, blogging, or constructing a seminar. The options are endless. You have something. Do not waste it. Do not hide your gift. Let it shine. Discover it and do it!

Matthew 5:15 – *Nor do people light a lamp and put it under a basket, but on a stand, and it gives light to all in the house.*

We are all inspired by people such as Warren Buffett, Bill Gates, Oprah Winfrey, and many others. We like to hear how people became successful. We also desire to become successful. You have what it takes to achieve success. You can inspire people. In order to do this, you must work hard at your craft. Do not be lazy in your business. Don't just work hard for money; work hard so that people can look at you, your effort, and your results, and be inspired.

Romans 12:11 – *Do not be slothful in zeal, be fervent in spirit, serve the Lord.*

Character

Titus 2:7-8 – *Show yourself in all respects to be a model of good works, and in your teaching show integrity, dignity, and sound speech that cannot be condemned, so that an opponent may be put to shame, having nothing evil to say about us.*

Ephesians 5:8 – *for at one time you were darkness, but now you are light in the Lord. Walk as children of light*

Your character says a great deal about you. Carry and present yourself as a joyous, respectable, standup person. We should stand out in this regard. People should notice the life you live. Has anyone ever affected your life in a positive way? Have you ever taken note of someone's smiling, content, or generous nature?

I remember one such person. One day, when I was a little kid, I scrounged up some money and hiked over to a fast food restaurant nearby. I ordered the food, but as I prepared to pay, I realized I did not have enough money. As I told the lady I needed to change my order, an elderly gentleman pulled out some money and paid for my meal. I thanked him but told him that I could just order something else. He, however, insisted on paying. He smiled and told me that all he asked was that I do the same for someone else when I had money.

I never forgot that gentleman, although he may have completely forgotten about this event an hour later. Unfortunately, I won't get the chance to explain to him how much his generosity changed my outlook. What he gave me that day was worth more than the $5 meal. His small gesture made an everlasting impression on me and I pray that I can keep the cycle going. You never know who you might affect. Even a small gesture can go a long way. Someone could be contemplating something disastrous. Your seemingly small gesture could be enough to deter him/her.

Become a "people person"—someone who, generally, gets along with most people. Such persons always seem happy. They are very friendly and they get along with people because they possess many positive characteristics. These characteristics, such as being kind, are taught in the Bible as seen below:

Ephesians 4:32 – Be kind to one another, tender-hearted, forgiving one another, as God in Christ forgave you.

Romans 12:10 – Love one another with brotherly affection. Outdo one another in showing honor.

Matthew 5:7 – Blessed are the merciful, for they shall receive mercy.

I John 4:7 – Beloved, let us love one another, for love is from God, and whoever loves has been born of God and knows God.

II Peter 1:5-7 – For this very reason, make every effort to supplement your faith with virtue, and virtue with knowledge, and knowledge with self-control, and self-control with steadfastness, and steadfastness with godliness, and godliness with brotherly affection, and brotherly affection with love.

Give encouragement. Constructive criticism can be necessary at times, but do not always criticize and look for flaws. A few positive experiences can outweigh many negative experiences. People are attracted to encouraging, supportive people.

I Thessalonians 5:11 – *Therefore encourage one another and build one another up, just as you are doing.*

Hebrews 10:24-25 – *And let us consider how to stir up one another to love and good works, not neglecting to meet together, as is the habit of some, but encouraging one another, and all the more as you see the day drawing near.*

Be honest in your dealings. People will need to rely on you at some point. Prove to be trustworthy. Do not be one of those people who like to lie for no reason. We all know someone like that. Don't deceive to get ahead. Be genuine; it will help you much more than being underhanded will. People will recognize and respect you for your honest dealings.

Deuteronomy 5:20 – *And you shall not bear false witness against your neighbor.*

Matthew 5:37 – *Let what you say be simply "Yes" or "No"; anything more than this comes from evil.*

I John 2:21 – *I write to you, not because you do not know the truth, but because you know it, and because no lie is of the truth.*

Be interested in people. If you want to be interesting to someone, take interest in what that person is interested in. Learn people's names. Being able to remember names is a common characteristic of highly successful people. Listen to people's stories. The only thing people love more than talking about themselves is having someone who will listen to them talk about themselves. Sometimes, people really need that helpful ear; give it to them. They may need to vent and get something off their chest. When people tell you about their problems, most of the time, they are not looking for your advice. Rather, they just want a listening ear.

Matthew 11:15 – *He who has ears to hear, let him hear.*

Listening to people makes you privy to how they feel. This world would be a much better place if we would all be more empathetic. See through the eyes of others. Walk in their shoes. Feel what they feel. This will allow you to understand why someone does a certain thing or acts in a particular way. When you know why someone does something, you can react better to that person and strategize a solution if need be.

There was once a student who would always sleep in class; every day was the same. This started to annoy the teacher to the point that he asked the student to stay after class. The teacher was planning on giving the student a good talking to. Before going in on the student, he decided to find out why he was sleeping every day. Was he trying to be disrespectful? Did he not understand the material?

As it turned out, the student's single mother had recently lost her job. The student was working well into the night to put food on the table for his mother and younger siblings. Had the teacher begun yelling and condemning the student without knowing why he was behaving that way, he could have made the situation worse. Perhaps that may even have been the straw that pushed the young man to drop out. Luckily, the teacher put himself in a position where he was able to help the student. This is all because he took the time to find out why. Take the time to be empathetic and see where other people are coming from. Feel what they feel. Walk a mile in their shoes.

Romans 12:15 – *Rejoice with those who rejoice, weep with those who weep.*

Taking a few minutes to assess the situation gave that teacher the tools to be an asset and prevented him from doing something detrimental. We all get angry; it is human nature. However, if we allow that anger to direct our feelings, it usually leads to us doing something we will regret. It is okay to be angry; just don't let that anger make decisions for you. Take a few seconds to think things through rationally.

Ephesians 4:26 – *Be angry and do not sin; do not let the sun go down on your anger*

Proverbs 15:1 – *A soft answer turns away wrath, but a harsh word stirs up anger.*

Realize that you represent more than just you. You represent your friends, family, job, school, church, and even God. Make people talk well about them. Make people talk well about you. Be a person with standards and integrity. When people see you, they should see an aspect of God.

I Timothy 4:12 - *Let no one despise you for your youth, but set the believers an example in speech, in conduct, in love, in faith, in purity.*

This world is looking for an example of success. People need someone to show them the way to act, work, and be respectful. Be that example. Jesus said you are the salt of the world. Give this world a little flavoring. Let your light shine brightly like the star you are.

Matthew 5:13-14 – _You are the salt of the earth, but if salt has lost its taste, how shall its saltiness be restored? It is no longer good for anything except to be thrown out and trampled under people's feet. You are the light of the world. A city set on a hill cannot be hidden._

10 THE SEVEN BIBLICAL KEYS TO SUCCESS

We all want to be successful in our endeavors. How can you become successful? Are there keys to being successful? And if so, what are they? If you speak to those who have achieved success in their lives, you will notice that they mention similar ingredients for that success. The fact of the matter is that there is a recipe for success. There are seven biblical keys to success. These keys are as follows:

1. Have a vision
2. Make a plan
3. Pray for success
4. Have faith
5. Educate yourself
6. Put in the work
7. Endure until the end

Have a Vision

Every invention, book, movie, song, etc. started with an idea or thought. It is impossible for a thing to be created without it first being thought up. That sounds obvious, but sometimes we miss the obvious. We need to think of what we want to pursue.

God made us all creative creatures. There are treasures in our minds; we just have to unlock those treasures. That means we need ideas. Everything started as an idea. Use your powerful mind to think up great ideas. Think of many ideas and choose the one with which you are most comfortable. You can brainstorm ideas with friends, family, and business partners.

When that thought becomes an idea that you want to pursue, keep that vision in your head and think about it daily. Think about the reason you want this idea to come to fruition. You can visualize it coming to pass. Visualizing is a common tool used in many industries, including sports. Athletes are taught to envision themselves catching the ball and scoring a touchdown. Visualizing puts you in the correct mindset for your tasks. It minimizes nervousness and makes the task much more manageable. When you are put in a certain situation, visualizing enables you to know what to do. You will recall what was needed in order to achieve success. Visualizing is a type of practice. It prepares you for the real thing.

When you have a vision, remember it is *your* vision. Most other people will not be able to see your vision. People thought the Wright brothers were crazy for trying to create a flying machine. Remember, too, that Henry Ford was told by his engineers that the Model T was not plausible. Neither the Wright brothers nor Ford let those people stop them. Do not let people talk down about your vision. A vision is a necessity for success. Have a vision.

Proverbs 29:18 – Where there is no vision, the people perish...

Make a Plan

Luke 14:28 – For which of you, desiring to build a tower, does not first sit down and count the cost, whether he has enough to complete it?

In the above verse, which I have previously referenced, Jesus is pointing out the seemingly obvious — making a plan is essential for success. A plan keeps you on track. It tells you where to go. Without a plan, you are going blindly toward your goal. In football, you make a game plan to defeat your opponent. You look at the various factors that will lead you to success and the ones that won't. Then you figure out how to implement the former and eliminate the latter. This is what we must do with all our undertakings.

It is impossible to achieve success without a plan. Steve Jobs had a plan for what he wanted to do with Apple. He followed through with that plan and soon turned Apple into a global powerhouse. If you look at any sports team that has won a championship, the coach or manager had to put together a plan to win that championship. You, too, must make a plan for success.

Proverbs 14:8 – *The wisdom of the prudent is to discern his way: but the folly of fools is deceiving.*

Pray for Success

Philippians 4:6 – *do not be anxious about anything, but in everything by prayer and supplication with thanksgiving let your requests be made known to God.*

Prayer is simply talking to God. The scripture above suggests incorporating prayer into everything. This includes our personal projects. The Bible is filled with stories of people praying that their undertakings will be successful. This list includes Abraham, Jacob, Moses,

David, Nehemiah, Jesus, Paul, and many more. Prayer not only gets God involved, but it also provides us with psychological comfort. Anxiousness can cause mistakes and lead to failure. People perform better when they are in a calm state of mind and are thinking clearly. This is what Paul is alluding to in Philippians 4:6.

God wants to bless us. However, if you want something, you must ask. We are told if we ask, we will be answered; if we seek, we will find. Prayer is a powerful tool if we incorporate it into our tasks. Pray and ask for success.

Luke 11:9 – And I tell you, ask, and it will be given to you; seek, and you will find; knock, and it will be opened to you.

James 5:16 – The prayer of a righteous person has great power as it is working.

Have Faith and Believe

Mark 11:24 – Therefore I tell you, whatever you ask in prayer, believe that you have received it, and it will be yours.

Mark 11:24 is one of my favorite scriptures. The advice Jesus is giving us here is golden: You must believe that you will receive the thing you pray for; it is then that you will have it. People often wonder why some of their prayers go unanswered. It may be because they truly do not believe. The person who does not believe he can do a thing will never do that thing.

Matthew 17:19-20 – *Then the disciples came to Jesus privately and said, "Why could we not cast it out?" He said to them, "Because of your little faith. For truly, I say to you, if you have faith like a grain of mustard seed, you will say to this mountain, 'Move from here to there,' and it will move, and nothing will be impossible for you."*

Truly believing in your God-given abilities is not always easy. In fact, a fair number of people in society doubt their abilities. This is common and happens to us all. When doubt and fear start to arise, you must trump them with faith. You must do so thoroughly and rigorously. If necessary, ask God to help your unbelief. Ask him to give you the necessary faith required to complete your task.

Mark 9:24 – *Immediately the father of the child cried out and said, "I believe; help my unbelief!"*

Faith, or the lack thereof, can make or break our endeavors. With faith, we have the ability to do things that we otherwise could not imagine. Whenever you begin a project, believe and know that success is within your grasp.

Mark 9:23 – *And Jesus said to him, "'If you can'! All things are possible for one who believes."*

Take Action

While faith is necessary for success, it is nothing without action. We can believe we will be successful all we want. If we do not take action toward completing our task, we will never finish. If a student does not go to class, he/she will not pass the class. I can believe in my writing skills, but if I do not actually sit down and write this book, it will never be completed. Faith without works is dead.

James 2:26 – *For as the body apart from the spirit is dead, so also faith apart from works is dead.*

If you truly believe, then you will take action. You actually show your faith by taking action; in fact, you cannot show your faith without taking action. If you believe you can accomplish something that you want, then you will take the necessary action steps to get it done. Otherwise, you are just all talk. True faith requires action.

James 2:18 – *But someone will say, "You have faith and I have works." Show me your faith apart from your works, and I will show you my faith by my works.*

Ordinary or minimum action will not cut it. Your goals should be aggressively pursued. Too many times, we start a project only to not give it our all. How many successful people do you know who gave minimal effort? Work hard. Put your heart into it. Hard work breeds success. The diligent are rewarded.

Proverbs 28:19 – *Whoever works his land will have plenty of bread, but he who follows worthless pursuits will have plenty of poverty.*

Proverbs 13:4 – *The soul of the sluggard craves and gets nothing, while the soul of the diligent is richly supplied.*

Colossians 3:23 – *Whatever you do, work heartily, as for the Lord and not for men*

Educate Yourself

Education is important. You cannot be successful without becoming educated in your field. Warren Buffett knows the ins and outs of investing. Peyton Manning knows how to read and dissect a defense. Famous heart surgeon Ben Carson knows the anatomy of the human heart. Chess master Bobby Fischer knew the intricacies of the game. You must also become an expert in your field. Seek to know more than the average Joe. Seek to know more than your competition. Study and become a guru at your craft.

Proverbs 23:12 – *Apply your heart to instruction and your ear to words of knowledge.*

Everyone wants to be successful; but not everyone will attain the knowledge necessary to do so. This separates the hungry from the ordinary. Obstacles become larger when you are not properly educated. Education brings you closer to success. A big reason why people fail is that they didn't educate themselves about their craft.

Hosea 4:6 – *My people are destroyed for lack of knowledge*

Proverbs 1:7 – *The fear of the Lord is the beginning of knowledge; fools despise wisdom and instruction.*

No one starts off as an expert. Until you become an expert (and even after), you can seek advice from those who have achieved success. Having a mentor is a good idea. Jesus was a mentor to his disciples. He taught them what he knew. Elijah mentored Elisha. Thomas Edison mentored Henry Ford. Famed NFL coach Mike Shanahan was mentored by three-time Super Bowl-winning NFL coach Bill Walsh. Like these men, you can learn from those who have done it before. Surround yourself with knowledgeable people. You do not have to reinvent the wheel; just learn from someone who has built it before. Educate yourself.

Proverbs 1:5 – *Let the wise hear and increase in learning, and the one who understands obtain guidance,*

Endure Until the End

Never give up. There will be obstacles, naysayers, and challenges thrown at us. This is definite. When they come, keep moving. When situations change, do not be a fish out of water; learn to be a bird. Regroup, re-strategize, and adapt. Keep plotting your next course of action. Eat the elephant one bite at a time. If you keep putting a string of victories together, then eventually, battle by battle, you will win the war. Do not be one of those people who give up right before their success comes. Exhaust all your options. Go until you cannot go anymore, and then go a little further. Only the strong survive.

These are the keys the Bible gives us that will lead to success. Have a vision. Make a plan to make that vision come to fruition. Hold tight to that vision. Pray for success and believe you will achieve your goal. Carry out the steps aggressively and work hard. Study and become an expert in your field. Weather the storms that will come and endure until the end. It is then, and only then, that you will be successful.

Matthew 24:13 – *But the one who endures to the end will be saved.*

Galatians 6:9 – *And let us not grow weary of doing good, for in due season we will reap, if we do not give up.*

11 WOLVES

Matthew 7:15 – *Beware of false prophets, who come to you in sheep's clothing but inwardly are ravenous wolves.*

When I was younger, I was shorter than most of my peers. Because of this, when I played basketball, I was not much of a rebounder. Instead, I would try to steal the ball. One technique I would use was to try to sneak behind the dribbler and steal the ball. Whenever anyone would try this in organized ball, the dribbler's teammates would yell "wolf!" to alert the dribbler that someone was trying to steal the ball from behind.

What do people mean when they describe someone as a wolf? Usually, a wolf is someone who practices deception and manipulation. He/she comes across as a good person, but has a secret agenda and uses others to advance his/her personal gain.

Wolves are everywhere. You can turn on the news and see segments about wolves every day. There are wolves at schools, churches, your job, the bank, insurance companies, phone companies, etc. Wolves have been employed as pastors, evangelists, politicians, professors, lawyers, policemen, life coaches, and journalists; literally, every walk of life has seen a wolf or two.

I personally know of a successful life coach who is nothing more than a wolf. It is sad because these people are good at getting you to trust them. They pretend they are looking out for your best interest, while really trying to drain you of all the money they possibly can. They are leaches.

One thing wolves do is learn what will work and what will not. This leads to a regurgitation of material on their part. They rename and repackage the same information in order to draw you in. Often, what they are offering is a product, book, or information that you can find elsewhere. However, they are looking for the weak, the gullible, and the misinformed.

Have you ever seen a predator hunt? It does not matter if it is a wolf, lion, cheetah, or another animal. The predator usually goes after the weakest, slowest prey. This makes the hunt easier and increases the chance of success. People are the same way. Bullies usually go after the easiest targets. So do the wolves out there.

The goal of those predators is not just to kill the gazelle, deer, rabbit, or other prey. The goal is to have something to eat for dinner. In the same manner, the goal of the wolf is not to rip you off or put you in a bad predicament. Rather, the wolf's goal is to build up as much wealth as possible. The problem is that he/she will cheat, lie, and deceive you in order to do that.

We each have our own agenda. It does not matter what it is, but everyone does indeed have an agenda. That does not mean everyone is bad or selfish. Some people's agendas are to truly help others out, do a good job, and do good works. A father's agenda may be to provide for his family. A doctor's agenda may be to heal people. However, it is because of the fact that people have their own agenda that we should keep our eyes open.

II Timothy 3:1-5 – But understand this, that in the last days there will come times of difficulty. For people will be lovers of self, lovers of money, proud, arrogant, abusive, disobedient to their parents, ungrateful, unholy, heartless, unappeasable, slanderous, without self-control, brutal, not loving good, treacherous, reckless, swollen with conceit, lovers of pleasure rather than lovers of God, having the appearance of godliness, but denying its power. Avoid such people.

Most people certainly are not wolves. Despite this, it is a good idea to keep your eyes open and try to determine their motive. Again, their motive might be benevolent. We are just trying to beware of the wolves in sheep's clothing—the people who will deceive and devour us. Believe me, they are out there.

I Peter 5:8 – Be sober-minded; be watchful. Your adversary the devil prowls around like a roaring lion, seeking someone to devour.

There is not much more to say in this chapter besides be aware. This chapter is short, but important. Keep your eyes open. Do not be a victim. Do not be gullible. Do your research. It is a good idea to get a second opinion on things. Ask your friends and family what they think. You might become enamored with a product or person, which might lead you to make the wrong decision. A few extra trustworthy, reliable eyes can prevent you from making a mistake and give you peace of mind regarding the decisions you make.

<u>Proverbs 11:14</u> – Where there is no guidance, a people falls, but in an abundance of counselors there is safety.

12 THE ENEMY

Who is your enemy? Who is your opponent? We always seem to be in competition. Our success is often characterized by how we compare to others. There are those out there who will want you to fail. However, we all have only one true enemy.

Naysayers are a part of our everyday life. Whenever you attempt to move ahead, there will be those who hate it. They despise the fact that you even have dreams and goals. You will be told that your aspirations are unrealistic, difficult, childish, and a waste of time. But these naysayers cannot stop you from reaching your goal. As a matter of fact, having naysayers is a good thing; it means you are attempting something worthwhile. The more you try to progress, the more people will try to dissuade you. Even Jesus had his fair share of naysayers. In a way, having naysayers and haters can be a status symbol. People hate for a reason. If you were not doing anything worthwhile, there would be little reason for one to hate on you. You are blessed when people speak against you.

Matthew 5:11 – *Blessed are you when others revile you and persecute you and utter all kinds of evil against you falsely.*

John 15:21 – *But all these things they will do to you on account of my name, because they do not know him who sent me.*

John 15:18 – *If the world hates you, know that it has hated me before it hated you.*

Naysayers only have power over us if we give it to them. Far too many times, we believe what they have to say. Remember that their words are just that—words. What people say can discourage you, but it cannot truly stop you. They are not God. What they say does not count. At times, it may seem like they have defeated you, but you are not defeated until you give up. While they may oppose us, naysayers are not our one true enemy because they cannot stop us.

Competitors, too, are a part of our everyday life. There are people attempting the same thing as you; it makes sense to us that we compete against them. The Cubs compete against the Cardinals. Yahoo competes with Google. At work, you compete against rival companies and, at times, even against your own coworkers.

It is easy to see these people as our opponents. We think we need to outsell the other salesmen, give a better deal, and outthink the next man. However, the bar is only set at our competitors if we choose to limit ourselves by leaving it there. Do you think the likes of Warren Buffett, Mark Zuckerberg, Steve Jobs, and Oprah Winfrey limited themselves to just being better than their competition? They do not set the bar at just being better than the next person. They strive to reach levels that no one else has. You, too, do not have to limit yourself to simply being better than your competitor. The bar is only set where you allow it to be set. Since our competitors do not set our bar, then our competitors are not our one true enemy either.

Still, there are some people who see the devil as the true enemy. When things go wrong in our lives, we like to cast blame. For the last 6,000 years of human history, the devil has often been the target of said blame. It is easy to blame our problems on the devil. We dichotomize things into a battle between the forces of good and the forces of evil, with the devil being the headman in charge of the forces of evil. Therefore, he must be our one true enemy.

Is this really the case? Not really. Like the naysayers and competitors, the devil cannot truly stop you. He can only stop you if you let him. What we perceive is very important. If you think the devil is defeating you, then you will be defeated. However, if you keep going, then he cannot truly stop you. Jesus said that he has already overcome the world and that what is in you is greater than anything the world can throw at you. You will not have more than you can bear. Knowing this, we must conclude that the devil is not our one true enemy.

John 16:33 – I have said these things to you, that in me you may have peace. In the world you will have tribulation. But take heart; I have overcome the world.

I John 5:4 – For everyone who has been born of God overcomes the world. And this is the victory that has overcome the world— our faith.

So if the naysayers, competitors, or even the devil is not our one true enemy, then who is? Maybe you have guessed it already. The answer is you. You are your biggest opponent. You are the only person who can make you quit. The Bible talks about the lust of the eye, the lust of the flesh, and the pride of life. These qualities that bring us down are qualities within you.

I John 2:16 – For all that is in the world—the desires of the flesh and the desires of the eyes and pride of life—is not from the Father but is from the world.

We sabotage ourselves far too often. Instead of putting in the necessary extra hours, we take a break. We turn on the television or surf the Internet. Our ten-minute nap turns into an hour. We give in to what the flesh wants. We would rather be entertained now than to finish and rest later. Success requires time, effort, work, sweat. Do not kill yourself through laziness. Put in the work now and reap the rewards later.

Proverbs 6:9-11 – How long will you lie there, O sluggard? When will you arise from your sleep? A little sleep, a little slumber, a little folding of the hands to rest, and poverty will come upon you like a robber, and want like an armed man.

II Corinthians 9:6 – The point is this: whoever sows sparingly will also reap sparingly, and whoever sows bountiful will also reap bountifully.

We hurt ourselves through our excessive complaining. We have all complained about something or someone. Complaining, though, is not the way to solve a problem.

Only action will do that. Worrying is the same; it does nothing except take up precious time. Do not waste your time obsessing. If you have a problem, then either take action to improve it or ignore it and move on.

Sometimes we get scared of what others might say and/or think. This fear can prevent us from even attempting to achieve a goal. But your fear is your fault, not theirs. You are the one who is scared and letting that fear stop you. Do you think Michael Jordan listened to the people who said he could not make it? People's words are only words. It is your responsibility not to be deterred by them.

Stay committed and focused on your goal. How many times have we all started something only to lose steam and give up? How many times have you postponed your work for another day? Procrastination only produces less than your best. There have been times when I have waited until the last moment to do work. I have had students give me work that is sub-par compared to their competency level because they waited until the last few days to begin. Utilize your time properly. Press on.

Our desire to please ourselves is powerful. The problem is that this desire leads us to take a route that does not ultimately benefit us. We look for instant gratification.

We want to be pleased now. We like things to be easy, and sometimes it seems easier to give up than to keep going. Sometimes it seems easier to quit than to face people's ridicule. Giving up is easy; quitting is simple. Just remember though: Giving up and quitting never leads to success—only to failure.

II Chronicles 15:7 – But you, take courage! Do not let your hands be weak, for your work shall be rewarded.

No one can make you quit or give up. That includes the naysayers, competitors, opponents, devil, haters, your family, or anyone and everything else we blame. This includes death. Think about that: Death may prevent you from fully realizing your goal, but it cannot make you quit. Only you can make you quit. That is why you are your one true enemy. Compete with yourself. Keep trying to outperform and surprise yourself. Turn your biggest enemy into your biggest ally. Know that no one can stop you. You are powerful.

13 YOU ARE POWERFUL

Have you ever felt that, in the grand scheme of things, you are not that important? We have all felt this way at some point. You look around at the billions of people on the planet and you feel small. You are just one insignificant person; what you do does not really matter that much. As it turns out, you are important, significant, and powerful.

Matthew 23:10 – *Neither be called instructors, for you have one instructor, the Christ.*

In the above verse, Jesus tells his disciples not to be called or call anyone master or instructor (depending on your Bible version). He is saying that you are not better than anyone. On the flip side, this also means that no one is better than you. Yes you have superiors, bosses, and others in positions of authority, and you should respect them; but they are not better than you. Keep that in mind. If Jesus implies that no one is better than you, then you can take that to the bank.

We were made powerful beings. God gave us the ability to create. Look at some of the accomplishments of mankind. We have created the atomic bomb and the Internet, walked on the moon, put a rover on Mars, and invented ice cream. Technology is improving every day. The human race is a marvelous thing. You are a marvelous being. If we have God on our side, nothing can stop us. Nothing is impossible.

Luke 1:37 – For nothing will be impossible with God.

John 14:14 – If you ask me anything in my name, I will do it.

Jesus is, perhaps, the most revered man in human history. This great man taught us that we, too, are great. He called us his friends. A friend is someone who cares about you—someone you can talk to when you need to. I don't know about you, but this makes me feel important. If the U.S. President were our friend, then that is something we would feel proud of, and maybe even brag about. What about the likes of Jesus being our friend?

John 15:15 – No longer do I call you servants, for the servant does not know what his master is doing; but I have called you friends, for all that I have heard from my Father I have made known to you.

Jesus did many great things. We, too, can do great things. Jesus even said that we can do greater things than he did. The Bible is full of stories of men doing great things: David, Solomon, Paul, et al. Peter even walked on water. Why, then, do we feel inadequate? It has been said that our biggest fear is not that we are inadequate, but that we are powerful beyond belief. It is easy to live the life of someone inadequate, but the thought of living the life of a powerful man or woman makes us feel uneasy. Even more than that, the fear and embarrassment of trying and failing causes many people to not even attempt to achieve their goal. If you want to walk on water, then you have to get out of the boat. Do not be afraid of your greatness.

Proverbs 29:25 – The fear of man lays a snare, but whoever trusts in the Lord is safe.

Isaiah 41:10 – Fear not, for I am with you; be not dismayed, for I am your God; I will strengthen you, I will help you, I will uphold you with my righteous right hand.

If you take a look at science, the odds of us becoming life are actually against us. One small change could have resulted in another seed being fertilized. The fact that you are here means that you are important. You have overcome a great deal just to be born. You have this life for a reason. God knew us when we were in the womb. We started as a thought in God's infinite mind. If God indeed does not make a mistake, then you were meant to be here. You have a God-given purpose.

Jeremiah 1:5 – *"Before I formed you in the womb I knew you, and before you were born I consecrated you; I appointed you a prophet to the nations."*

God made you in his image, after his likeness. We are children of God. All children have traits of their parents. You, too, have traits of God in you. Some people go as far as to claim that they, too, are gods. They argue that an orange can only produce an orange. Therefore, God can only produce more of himself. I certainly do not claim to be a god. I do, however, acknowledge that I am of God; I come from God.

Genesis 1:26 – *Then God said, "Let us make man in our image, after our likeness..."*

Romans 8:16 – *The Spirit himself bears witness with our spirit that we are children of God*

John 1:12 – But to all who did receive him, who believed in his name, he gave the right to become children of God

I John 3:1 – See what kind of love the Father has given to us, that we should be called children of God; and so we are...

This is not a metaphor. This is literal. Our DNA has the greatness of God in it. Our solar system is made from a collapsed, imploded giant star. The remains of this star eventually created our Sun, the Earth, and the other planets in our solar system. The stardust remnants were filled with life-creating elements, such as nitrogen, carbon, hydrogen, oxygen, and others. Over the course of many years of being void and without form, our solar system began to take shape. Life on Earth was created. The years saw many changes, until we reached the point we are at today. This is science and it does not contradict the Bible.

Why do I mention this? Because we are made of that imploded star. We are a carbon-based life-form. The carbon from which we are made came from that star. The oxygen we breathe came from that star. We are literally stars. The same material that God used to make the moon, the sun, Jupiter, Saturn, Orion, Pleiades, Arcturus, etc. is the same material in us. When you look up at the heavens, realize that, in a way, you are looking up at an extension of yourself.

Genesis 1:1 – *In the beginning, God created the heavens and the earth.*

Genesis 2:7 – *then the Lord God formed the man of dust from the ground and breathed into his nostrils the breath of life, and the man became a living creature.*

Job 9:9-10 – *who made the Bear and Orion, the Pleiades and the chambers of the south; who does great things beyond searching out, and marvelous things beyond number.*

You are far from being insignificant, weak, and unimportant. God thought about you when he created you. He had you in mind for a reason. You are his child. He loves you and wants you to be successful. The next time you are feeling down, insignificant, or weak, step outside and look at nature. Gaze up at the night sky and realize that you truly are a powerful being created by the same God who created the universe. You are powerful. Be the star that God created you to be.

14 NEVER LEAVE YOU NOR FORSAKE YOU

There are times when we all have felt down in the dumps. We have all been lonely. Sometimes we feel like no one understands us. We contemplate what we are truly doing with our lives. We ask ourselves, What's the point? We have even felt like giving up and throwing in the towel. Peace is desired one way or another.

Negative feelings become so commonplace that they numb our lives. These feelings can often get the best of us. They take a toll on our physical lives and adversely impact our health. However, it is important to realize that even when you feel alone, you are never truly alone. God is always with you.

Matthew 28:20 – teaching them to observe all that I have commanded you. And behold, I am with you always, to the end of the age.

Many of us have heard the story of the footprints in the sand: There were two sets of footprints—God's and ours. During the rough, trying times of our lives, there was only a single set of footprints. We asked God where he was during the times that we needed him the most. God answered that the single set of footprints was when he was carrying us through those tough times. He said he would never leave us nor forsake us.

Deuteronomy 31:6 – Be strong and courageous. Do not fear or be in dread of them, for it is the Lord your God who goes with you. He will not leave you or forsake you.

Joshua 1:5 – No man shall be able to stand before you all the days of your life. Just as I was with Moses, so I will be with you. I will not leave you or forsake you.

Some of us try to ignore our feelings and problems in the hope that they will eventually go away. Some of them might actually go away with time, but unless we address them, they will return. When we meet our problems head-on, we will be stronger. Our problems provide us with patience, experience, and hopeful confidence.

Romans 5:3-4 – *More than that, we rejoice in our sufferings, knowing that suffering produces endurance, and endurance produces character, and character produces hope*

We do not have to try to fix these problems by ourselves. We have help. Praying really can be a difference maker. Whenever you have a problem, bring it to the big man upstairs. Pray; it changes things.

Psalm 55:22 – *Cast your burden on the Lord, and he will sustain you; he will never permit the righteous to be moved.*

Matthew 11:28-30 – *Come to me, all who labor and are heavy laden, and I will give you rest. Take my yoke upon you, and learn from me, for I am gentle and lowly in heart, and you will find rest for your souls. For my yoke is easy, and my burden is light.*

Philippians 4:7 – *And the peace of God, which surpasses all understanding, will guard your hearts and your minds in Christ Jesus.*

Sometimes our problems seem too much for us to handle. We come close to completely breaking down. Think about this though: Despite all of the hell you have been through in your life, if you are reading this, then you have not been defeated. Again, I will repeat: IF YOU ARE READING THIS, THEN YOU HAVE NOT BEEN DEFEATED! You are still standing and you still have a fighting chance! You can triumph because God said he will not give you more than you can bear. Essentially, God is saying that you can overcome ANY situation life throws at you. If God believes you can overcome a situation, then you can!

I Corinthians 10:13 – *No temptation has overtaken you that is not common to man. God is faithful, and he will not let you be tempted beyond your ability, but with the temptation he will also provide the way of escape, that you may be able to endure it.*

The problem is that many of us want relief right now. That relief will come sooner than later with the right mentality, attitude, action, resolve, and fortitude. We should do all we can possibly do to better our situation. When you have exhausted all options, then wait on God to bring your next step to you. It will come.

Psalm 27:14 – *Wait for the Lord; be strong, and let your heart take courage; wait for the Lord!*

Isaiah 40:31 – *but they who wait for the Lord shall renew their strength; they shall mount up with wings like eagles; they shall run and not be weary; they shall walk and not faint.*

Psalm 46:10 – *"Be still, and know that I am God. I will be exalted among the nations, I will be exalted in the earth!"*

Fear can cause problems to be prolonged and worsened. We fear that we will fail. We are afraid that things may actually become worse, or at the very least, never get better. This limits our action and weakens our resolve. Fear, however, is just an emotion. Most of the time, what we fear will never come to fruition to the extent that we imagine. We usually picture something worse. What that does is hold us back. We are so afraid that we think it is better to not even try.

Fear will come; it is a part of life. When it does arise, work past it. Keep moving forward with your plans. Fear will not stop you unless you give in to it.

Psalm27:1 – The Lord is my light and my salvation; whom shall I fear? The Lord is the stronghold of my life; of whom shall I be afraid?

Psalm 91:5-7 – You will not fear the terror of the night, nor the arrow that flies by day, nor the pestilence that stalks in darkness, nor the destruction that wastes at noonday. A thousand may fall at your side, ten thousand at your right hand, but it will not come near you.

Develop the mindset that things will work out. Most of the time, they will. Have faith in yourself. More importantly, have faith in God's promise. He said he would never leave you nor forsake you. He also said he would protect and keep us. Walk in that promise.

Isaiah 41:13 – For I, the Lord your God, hold your right hand; it is I who say to you, "Fear not, I am the one who helps you."

Psalm 91:11 – For he will command his angels concerning you to guard you in all your ways.

Psalm 23:4 – Even though I walk through the valley of the shadow of death, I will fear no evil, for you are with me; your rod and your staff, they comfort me.

Our problems and negative situations have molded us into who we are and they will be a part of the person we become. We will all have problems and issues; the important thing is how we deal with them. You can let the problems keep you stagnant and bring you down, or you can seek out the lesson to be learned. Every situation has a solution and every problem has a lesson that can be learned. This is why problems can make us stronger. This is up to you though. Trust that all things, including problems, work together for good.

Romans 8:28 – And we know that for those who love God all things work together for good, for those who are called according to his purpose.

This world can be brutal. It is rough on everyone: the rich, the poor, Americans, Chinese, Christians, Muslims, Atheists, blacks, whites, Hispanics—everyone. However, this world can also be a great place; it should be a great place. Be determined that you will overcome any challenge just short of death. You can make the best of this life. The world and your problems are tough, but with God's help, you are tougher.

I John 4:4 – Little children, you are from God and have overcome them, for he who is in you is greater than he who is in the world.

The next time you feel beaten down by life, know that you are not alone in that feeling. There are others out there who are feeling just as bad as you do. Take me, for instance; at some point in my life, I have felt alone. I have felt that people could not understand me or my situation. I saw no light at the end of the tunnel. I have been upset at politicians and my country. I have been angered by religious people and religions in general. I have second-guessed God on more than one occasion. I did not understand how he could allow certain things to happen. I have contemplated his nature and if he even exists. I debated if it was even worth going on. Maybe oblivion was more peaceful. I have teetered on the edge.

One thing God showed me is that I was not the only person feeling that way. How do I know? Because there are people who go over the edge every day. God also showed me how to overcome this. In the Bible, there is a story of a starving widow who was running out of food during a famine. She planned on cooking her last meal for her and her son and, afterward, they would go and die. However, her food became plentiful after she cooked her last bit of food for someone else who was hungry.

I Kings 17:12-15 – *And she said, "As the Lord your God lives, I have nothing baked, only a handful of flour in a jar and a little oil in a jug. And now I am gathering a couple of sticks that I may go in and prepare it for myself and my son, that we may eat it and die." And Elijah said to her, "Do not fear; go and do as you have said. But first make me a little cake of it and bring it to me, and afterward make something for yourself and your son. For thus says the Lord, the God of Israel, 'The jar of flour shall not be spent, and the jug of oil shall not be empty, until the day that the Lord sends rain upon the earth.'" And she went and did as Elijah said. And she and he and her household ate for many days.*

That is how you overcome depression, money problems, and other negative situations—by helping those in situations that are similar to yours. If you are depressed, find a way to help someone else who is depressed. If you need money, look for a way to help someone less fortunate than you. If you need someone to smile at you, then go and smile at someone. If you need a hug, give someone a hug. This is the principle of reciprocation—give and it shall be given unto you.

Luke 6:38 – give, and it will be given to you. Good measure, pressed down, shaken together, running over, will be put into your lap. For with the measure you use it will be measured back to you.

If you help other people out, they will not be alone. You, too, will not be alone. No matter who helps you—or not—God will be there. He will always be by your side. Be strong in that promise. Be assertive about persevering through your problems. The problems can be rough, I know. They can pile up on you. Your situation can make you feel completely helpless. But you are not helpless; you have God on your side. And know that even though trouble may come at you from every side, you will not be distressed. You may become perplexed, but you will not despair. You may be persecuted, but you will not be abandoned. You will get knocked down, but you will never, ever be destroyed!

II Corinthians 4:8-9 – We are afflicted in every way, but not crushed; perplexed, but not driven to despair; persecuted, but not forsaken; struck down, but not destroyed

Romans 8:31 – What then shall we say to these things? If God is for us, who can be against us?

Isaiah 54:17 – no weapon that is fashioned against you shall succeed, and you shall confute every tongue that rises against you in judgment. This is the heritage of the servants of the Lord and their vindication from me, declares the Lord.

16 FINAL THOUGHTS

God provided us with tips to improve our life. This book is a compilation of some of those tips. It was intended to give you simple, practical advice and strategies to help you create a good life. Take what you learned and apply it to your life. If you do this, there is no doubt that you will see results. Here is a rundown of the book:

1. Adjust your thinking to match your goals. Think positively.
2. Be aggressive in your pursuits. Fight to eliminate laziness from your life.
3. Your body is a temple. Take care of it.
4. Maximize your productivity by managing your time.
5. Take time to enjoy your life. It is a gift from God.
6. Cheerfully give and gracefully receive.

7. Learn the rules of money. You control it; do not let it control you.

8. Use the seven biblical keys to achieve your goals.

9. Be quick to help and slow to judge. Learn to forgive.

10. Let your light shine. Be the example that people need.

11. Beware of those out there who would deceive, trick or cheat you.

12. Do not let yourself get in your way. Take responsibility for your life.

13. You are powerful and capable of great things.

14. Know that God is on your side. He will never leave you nor forsake you.

God gave us free will—the choice to do this or that. This is shown throughout the Bible time and time again. For example, Adam had the choice to listen to Eve. Peter had the choice to drop everything and follow Jesus. You, too, have the choice to live how you want to live. The choices you make affect your life. Sometimes they improve and enhance our lives; sometimes they hurt and weaken our lives.

You are in control of your life. You alone are responsible for the choices, strategies, and decisions that will improve our life. You can choose to live a boring, monotonous life, or you can choose to live an exciting, colorful life. You can choose to continue to struggle, or you can take measures to revitalize your life. Life is hard; we all go through trials and tribulations. You can let life beat you down, or you can decide that nothing will hold you back. The choice is yours. Today, you make the choice, the declaration, that you will have an enjoyable, productive, and worthwhile life! You will have a triumphant existence!

ACKNOWLEDGMENTS

Even though I am the author, without the help and support of others, this book could not have been completed. First, I want to thank God for blessing me with this life and for bringing these supportive people into my life. Here are some of those people:

To my family that I love – my wife Melanie Franklin, my parents John and Terri Franklin, my sister Ayanna Sortor, my brother Jameel Franklin, my brothers-in-law Darrin Sortor and Jake Mazuc, my niece Jayden Sortor, my nephew Jeremiah Sortor, my parents-in-law Kevin and Kim Mazuc, and my family in Indianapolis and beyond. I would like to especially thank my brother Trent Franklin and his company TF Creative Media. He did a great job promoting and designing the cover.

To the various organizations that had a hand in this book – Scribendi for doing a terrific editing job, Crossway Publications for allowing me to quote from their English Standard Version of the Holy Bible, Mt. Zion Apostolic Church (Springfield, IL and Indianapolis, IN), Kicknology for the inspiration, and my wonderful team at Triple Up Publications.

I would like to thank the wonderful friends and mentors that God has put in my life (both past and present) for their support: Eric Christopher Lee, Gavin Fry, the Sessi family (Quasivi, Patricia, Kolade, Kristin, Folarin), Adrian and Jessica Cummings, Jeremy and Britney Osborne, Josh Osborne, Jamie & Joe Etchill, Lawrence and Taylor Smith, Jackie Randall, Mike Rose, Vladimir St. Elien, Alex Alameda, Corey Johnson, Pastor Danny & Suzie Foster, Darryl Thomas, Jamartae Jackson, Jim Varner, Grant Stephenson, Steve Labozzetta, Daryl Chinn, Ricky Williams, Justin Jones, Cherrelle Brinker, Xiaodan Wang, Antoine Luster, Isaac Howdeshell, Dan Leatherman, Dr. Andrew Walsh, Dr. Jeff Crane, Dr. Laura Westhoff, Bridget Kramer, Emanuel Tilson, Alicia Stalcup, Chris Urban, Ted Harrison, Neal Taylor, Nick Pickett, Myron Flakes, Anthony Brigham, Dan Manuel, Jamie and Norma Jean Vargas, Katriel Ysrayl, and Uriah Israel.

I would also like to thank those who have inspired me indirectly. Even though I don't know them personally, each of them has contributed something to m life: Joseph Simmons, Pastor Joel Osteen, Hezekiah Walker, Brendan Burchard, Dave Ramsey, Deepak Chopra, Clifford Harris, Kobe Bryant, Peyton Manning, Warren Buffett, Martin Luther King Jr., Malcolm X, Mother Theresa, W.E.B. DuBois, Bill Gates, President Barak Obama, Paulo Coelho, Shawn Carter, Kirk Franklin, Bishop TD Jakes, Fred Hammond, Dr. Cornel West, Dr. Boyce Watkins, Reza Aslan, Oprah Winfrey, Andre Benjamin, John Hope Bryant, and Reverend Michael Beckwith.

Finally to the readers, I want to thank you for reading this book. I sincerely hope that you were able to take something away from this book! Remember you are powerful! Enjoy and make the most of this life. God bless.

ABOUT THE AUTHOR

Lee Franklin was born in Indianapolis, Indiana. He has lived in various states including Indiana, Illinois, Missouri, and Florida. Franklin graduated from Culver-Stockton College, where he majored in History and Political Science as well as played football for the Wildcats. He then went on to pursue his Masters in History Education at the University of Missouri St. Louis.

In 2011, Franklin went to Shenyang, Liaoning, China to teach at Shenyang Normal University. After teaching there for a few years, he has since returned to the States, where he continues to teach, write, and coach. Franklin is the Founder and CEO of Triple Up Publications – an organization dedicated to publishing inspirational material.

www.ingramcontent.com/pod-product-compliance
Lightning Source LLC
LaVergne TN
LVHW051414080426
835508LV00022B/3087